Treasures of the Heart

Charmaine Walker

authorHOUSE®

AuthorHouse™
1663 Liberty Drive
Bloomington, IN 47403
www.authorhouse.com
Phone: 1-800-839-8640

First published by AuthorHouse 01/22/2010

ISBN: 978-1-4490-1664-7 (sc)
ISBN: 978-1-4490-1665-4 (e)

Printed in the United States of America
Bloomington, Indiana

This book is printed on acid-free paper.

Content

INTRODUCTION

This book is dedicated to all the women around the world. *"To Thine Own Self Be True."*

Due to the explicit content inside this book, it is recommended for persons eighteen (18) years and over.

Women have always formed the backbone of any country or community, though they are not always lauded or recognized. Women are special beings who serve a special purpose. I believe in the whole notion of women empowering themselves. A woman's worth can and will never be able to be measured.

A woman has to realize that her body is her temple and thus should be honoured. Her soul is her strength, thus it should be protected. Her inner beauty is electrifying therefore it should be held in high regard. Women must realize true happiness can only come from within. No man or material objects can make us happy. There is no such thing as a soul mate or someone who can complete us. "It is a fallacy." As women, we should learn to appreciate who we are and never let anyone rob us of that privilege. To do other wise is letting someone or something take away our identity.

In today's 21st century world, women are still struggling to be seen as individuals or to be seen as equals just as men. In many instances, women are qualified but yet are barred from certain positions in companies or service clubs because they are women. In some countries, a woman cannot be Prime Minister or President. Those who may attain this level are often given a fight from male counterparts and their peers. Some women in the corporate world have had to become "Queen Bitches" in order to be seen, heard and not taken for granted.

Many countries around the world still view women as second class citizens. They are not allowed to speak out or ask questions in public without a man's present. Even some churches support the whole theory of women in submission. Thousands of women around the world suffer in silence from abuse in many forms or laws that suppress their "Civic rights."

One wonders if the whole role of women being on the same level with men will be seen world wide. It is like racism, though we make strides in getting rid of it, it is still present and alive. Every time we make global progress, something takes us back.

Treasures of a woman's heart are a number of short stories and poems written by different women including myself. Their names are withheld in order to protect their identities. The stories are about women's behaviour, thoughts, feelings and needs. The women are from different social classes, ethnic background and cultures. Women need a medium to be able to express themselves openly and honestly. They should not be criticized for doing so.

The title is appropriate because all women are treasures. We need to take time to love and pamper ourselves regardless of where we have been or what we have gone through. I hope some thoughts, stories or poems will touch someone from this book.

The Inevitable

There was screaming and shouting. Happy laughter, the sounds of little feet. Children, always a beauty to behold. But though such glorious noise was around me, my mind was far away...years away.

I was thinking of Dane. I still remember the first time I saw him I was only fifteen years old. I was with my friend, we lived in the same community and we were on holidays. We were coming from a friend's house and there came this red van beside us and offered us a ride. My friend Camille knew the driver, his name was Dane. He was full of chatter and laughter. I liked his sense of humour. He dropped us at our other friend's house, Lisa. When we got out, he said to Camille, "When am I going to see your friend again?" We both laugh and so did he. He drove off leaving a cloud of dust behind. I told Camille I liked him and asked who he was. She told me he was her sister's boyfriend.

The years came and went and I saw Dane more frequently about the place. We never really talked. I would always see him playing football. We lived in the same community in Portmore. Portmore was a large community with many different housing schemes. Everybody knew each other. The first time I watched Dane played football at the field, I had a good laugh. He was on top of his voice shouting and giving orders and running all over the place. He is a trip.

"Miss Walsh?" One of my students was calling me. "Can we eat now, and why are you laughing?" "Yes, you may eat." I replied. I did not realize I was laughing. I had taken my students out for the day. They wanted to eat so they could swim.

Dane's youngest son David came and put his arms around me. I asked him if he wanted pizza he said no he wanted 'A big Dads.' "What is that?" I asked. "You don't know?" He said with a surprise look on his face. "No", I said. He held out his hands and said "Hot dog." I grabbed him and tickled him and we both had a good laugh.

I made sure the children ate. They ate so fast, I thought they were going to choke. They all rushed to the pool, except David. Instead, he was quite contented to play in the yard. I went and found a seat right where I could keep an eye on them. Even though there were two life guards, they were still my responsibility. I looked at David stooping playing in the dirt with a poke man toy. He was oblivious of the others around him splashing and screaming. He resembled his father so much, his chubby cheeks and his feet turned in. He looked up at me, smiled and went back to what he was doing.

I thought of Jay, Dane's first child and his mother Kerry. We were not really friends but we spoke a lot. Actually, she was Camille's sister. The thing was, I had a weakness for people who were in need. In the later years to come, this same weakness was going to allow people to take advantage of me. I was somehow way above my peers, both those my age and older. They looked up to me and sought me for advice. My grandmother out of anger one day told me to become a psychologist. Well, ironically that's the path I am pursuing but more Child Psychology.

Well, Kerry had three children for three different men including Dane. Her life was not easy and her mother added to her stress. I use to offer to baby sit the children if she had to go somewhere, first to make peace between her mother and herself. Besides, my grandmother loved the children and I loved children.

Her son Jay was cheeky, he refused to go to my grandmother but he was so adorable you couldn't help but still like him. Kerry spoke to me a lot about her life. She was not happy. Funny how she spoke a lot about Dane, she seemed to have really liked him. I mostly listened to her because I thought that was what she needed most. Once she told me how Dane used to beat her and that's why she left him. I found this so hard to believe because he didn't strike me as that sort of person. Kerry didn't seem to have any luck with men.

I felt someone tugging at my pocket, I looked down and saw it was David; he was beside me showing me something. He gave me that incredible smile, he resembled both parents. He placed his hands on my knees and made a monkey face. I kissed him on his nose and we both laughed. I watched him as he ran off. Words cannot begin to explain the endless feelings I have for this child. I remembered how mad Kerry was when she found out Dane started talking to David's mother Cher. Cher actually lived behind Kerry. I didn't quite understand, but there seemed to have been some feud going on between both households. Kerry's mother, Miss Nicey didn't have anything good to say about Dane or Cher.

I also knew Cher from high school. Actually, I was a head of her. She usually moved with a particular crowd, not that they were bad or anything, just loud and aggressive. Cher was an attractive girl, quite, short and so she was nicknamed 'Half Pint.'

My eyes suddenly caught Killian trying to jump in the water. He was Dane's second child but Cher's first. He looked exactly like his mom. You were not allowed to jump in the water because it was quite shallow. This could cause an accident. I shouted, "Boy, you trying to kill yourself?" "Yes" he replied. "Do it when your parents are present" I said. He was a real cheeky little fellow. "I will just send my mummy to you because daddy is not going to trouble you" he said smiling. Of course I had to laugh, so did the other kids. "Get down" I said, wrinkling my brows, quite annoyed at the effect the Dane's men had on me even at eight years old.

I remember when Cher had Killian, she and Dane seem to have been quite fine. I would see them at parties or clubs, at that time in my life I went out quite a lot. Dane when he was with Cher never really spoke to anyone. He would just nod at you. I use to jokingly say he is under Cher's arrest. Kerry got her United States Visa and she told me she was not coming back and Jay would live with his father. I encouraged her not to go because at that time we were both working at a Radio Station. She was an Engineer and I produced the shows aired on Radio. I didn't see the need for her to run off and besides with the visa, she could come and go. She insisted that she needed to get away from everyone and everything.

I asked her even if it meant leaving her kids and she never answered. I never saw Kerry again after that last conversation.

Life went on; I got a job with the French Embassy in a section called Children Services where they provided different kinds of funding to children in third world countries. I really enjoyed this because I loved children so much. I had to do a lot of traveling locally, regionally and internationally. I had to work in children's home and schools. I saw healthy children, sick children, happy children, sad children, abused children. It was then I decided that I wanted a career in Child Psychology. I had already a Diploma in Special Education. I figured the two would be a good combination.

About a year and a half some things changed in my life, it became upside down. My grandparents separated this I couldn't understand after thirty years of marriage.

My grandmother just sold her house and moved to Miami. I just didn't get it. I always thought she was happy. Why uproot at this stage in your life. This affected me greatly because my grandparents meant a lot to me. Even though I was twenty four years old, I wasn't ready to see my grandparents who had become my parents hurting so much. Neither of them spoke about what happened. I moved to Kingston but moved back to Portmore. My friend's mother was migrating so she offered to rent me one of the rooms. I accepted, besides the rent was quite cheap and it was an opportunity to save.

I moved in with my girlfriend Kim whom I had known from I was eleven years old. It was okay but my mind was preoccupied with my grandmother. I visited her in Miami quite often. She seemed to be happy. I don't remember how or where but Dane showed up in my life. He told me it was over between him and Cher. Killian was just a baby at the time. Dane's grandmother had died and he was making all the funeral arrangements. We started spending a lot of time together. Every evening after work Dane would come and pick me up. He would take me all over while arranging for the funeral. I was his company. Most times we went back to his house. Dane was very good at hiding his feelings so I had no idea what he was going through. He and Cher had a lot of bitter quarrels. Once she ran her car into the back of his car. Dane didn't realize but he proved to be a distraction for me. The truth was we both provided different needs. Dane had a physical need and I an emotional need. When Dane talked about Cher, I listened. I never talked about my problems, he never asked. But I enjoyed Dane's company. There was just something about him that was exciting and I found him fascinating. I was drawn to him; I wasn't looking or expecting a relationship but I looked forward to spending my evenings with him.

The first time Dane slept with me there was nothing romantic about it. It was just sex, purely physical. This went on about three or four times. Once, Dane came for me in the middle of the night. It rained all night and Dane's house leaked. We didn't have sex and that night was quite different for me I liked it and I saw Dane from another perspective. In the morning when I woke, Dane told me I look ugly, we both laughed and I told him he was no prince. I enjoyed his sense of humor. He took me home and I didn't see him again for a week. When I saw Dane after that it was only for a short time. We didn't go back to his house; we stayed by me and fooled around. After Dane left that night, I didn't see him or heard from him for quite a while.

David now climbed into my lap. He snuggled in my arms and I held him close to my breast. I planted a kiss on his forehead and he smiled. His eyes began to close, he wanted to sleep. I felt a special connection to this child.

Four weeks past and it was obvious Dane had no intention of calling me. Then someone told me he and Cher were back together. I thought he could have at least said something, however I moved on. Two weeks after I felt dizzy constantly. Then I missed my period, I never dreamed or imagined that I could be pregnant. I thought I was just late. But one day while in the kitchen, I nearly fainted. I held on tightly to the cupboard. The sensation lasted about two minutes and then I went to lie down.

I was confused; I refuse to believe that I was pregnant. I told myself I am just sick. After all, I have not been eating properly. I will visit the doctor tomorrow after work. The next day at work, I could hardly function. The day moved quite slowly, at four o'clock I rushed out. The doctor's office was very full with patients waiting. Even though the room had air-conditioned, I was sweating profusely. It seemed like eternal before my name was called to see the doctor.

When I went in to Dr. Jones, we talked a bit. I explained to him that I haven't seen my period and that I was a bit anxious. He told me to calm down as this could be due to a number of reasons. He told me to lie down so that he could do a test. When Dr. Jones did this, he said my womb felt enlarge but this doesn't prove anything. I felt tense. He decided to do a pregnancy test which came out positive. Everything in the doctor's office began to go around, his lips were moving but I was not hearing a thing. "Pregnant" what was I going to do.? I sat down. Dr. Jones said, "Marci, you do have options." I explained everything to him about the father and his girlfriend.

Abortion was out of the question but how could I carry Dane's child. His girlfriend lived on the Avenue behind me; his first child's grandmother lived on the same road. My job because of its nature, forbid single women to become pregnant. If you did you were asked to give up the job. What did I get myself into? Besides, I had not seen or heard from Dane in weeks. David shifted in my arms and I held him tightly as I delve deeper in my thoughts. My doctor told me to think about it and get back to him. I didn't have much time because I was already six weeks. I decided to buy a ticket and go to Miami to spend the weekend. My grandmother was excited to see me, she sense something was wrong but she didn't pressure me to tell her. I was in a pensive mood through out the entire trip. I tried calling Dane twice but to no avail. I wondered what his reaction would be.

I went back home still uncertain as to what to do. While on the plane I remembered my grandmother telling me at the airport that whatever it was that was bothering me this too shall past. I thought to myself, how simple that sounded. Back home, I decided to take a walk. I was quite shock as to how tight my clothes seemed because I wasn't showing. But somehow I never realized the changes in my body. I just thought I was under stress because I never could imagine myself being in such a situation. I was so angry at myself. I fought back the tears. I took a walk to the end of the road. I stood there taking in everything and everyone around me. I saw two figures far from a distance, as they got closer, I realized that it was Cher and her friend, we all went to school together. But Cher was pregnant. I stood there my mouth open. They didn't see me and they turned on the next road. Something moved inside my stomach, I could barely walk home. I decided then and there I couldn't go on with this pregnancy. Dane surely had been busy. How could I bring a child in this complication? I also knew that my life along with my child would not be peaceful.

The next day, I scheduled an appointment to terminate my pregnancy. I didn't want my child to become part of a triangle, besides Dane and Cher would be given a chance to work at their relationship. I went in the doctor's office quite nervous. When I saw the doctor, he explained the entire procedure. I would be given four injections to prevent infection. I felt like I was a murderer, I wanted to run out of his office, so why weren't my feet moving?

I lay down and he started the procedure. I hated injection and I gave the doctor quite a hard time. It was painful. I got four injections, two in my bottom and two in my uterus. When it started poking inside me, it was the most excruciating pain I have ever felt. I felt as if I had been violated, all these instruments and tools going in and out of me. I clenched my fists and my teeth. I felt a tugged, I thought I was going to die and that was it. My baby was gone. I told him I wanted to see, but it was just pure blood, nothing was formed.

It was over. I felt hollow as I walked out of the doctor's office, a living dead. I felt invincible. I took my time to walk home, I felt lonely and invincible. I was bleeding profusely; the doctor gave me a whole pile of medication to take.

When I went home, I was happy not to see my girlfriend. I headed for the shower, I must have spent an hour just standing under the water trying to wash away the guilt and pain I was feeling. I crawled into my bed and stayed there for the next two weeks. I only got up to use the bathroom. I hardly ate, I told my girlfriend I was having the flu and she believed. I was grateful for her not questioning me. I took no calls, I cried in my pillows. Truth was, I wanted to die.

I could not hold back the tears, I saw the children all changed and running outside to play. I bit my lips until blood come and I hid my face in David's hair to hide my tears. David was still sleeping peacefully, the children didn't notice me, they began playing among themselves. I was glad for this because I did not want to answer their questions. I wiped my tears.

The years came and went and I never heard from Dane or saw him again. I hid behind church and buried myself in activities, dance and children services. I was now seeing someone. I got over Dane and I thought I was healed. I threw myself in my work and I became good at it. I developed a very strong love for children and I was constantly surrounded by children. The embassy I worked with pulled its funds out of Jamaica. It gave workers the option of transferring to another island or take a package. I took the package because I didn't want to leave; I had too many dreams to fulfill. I took the money I got and bought an apartment in Kingston. I was tired of Portmore, I wanted to get away and I did, at least that's what I thought.

A friend of mine was seeing someone who was the Principal of a Prep School. I was freelancing, I went in schools and gave workshops, seminars and started reading clubs and set up Resource Centres. I used up my skills learnt from the embassy, this was rare in Jamaica and so I became a consultant, but to be fully recognized, one needed a doctorate behind the name so I started my Master's in Education Psychology which would lead to doctorate. My girlfriend suggested I get in a school system and studied it for a while. So I went to Victoria Christian Academy where her friend was. I had no problem; the School Board was quite pleased with my experience and qualification. Victoria Christian Academy was a Christian school and they had a long list of rules, but what interested me was the curriculum, it was very unique.

Right away I started looking for a way to rewrite this North American Curriculum into the Jamaican system. The Resource Centre was in a mess and nobody had a clue about its purpose and it seemed there was some sort of stigma attached to it. So I rose to the challenged. I started working two and a half days while still keeping my other clients. I had plans to open up a Centre which has never been seen in this Country. The truth was, I hated Victoria Academy because they didn't practiced what they preached. I had a mission to accomplish so I shut out everything and everyone around and focused on what I had to do.

Things started to look up and I had won the confidence of the parents. I had a mixture of students, gifted, learning difficulties, dyslexia, and speech impediment. All of them did well. When they were tested, assessors were amazed they had completed two years work in one year. I felt good. This feeling was short lived.

One day while standing at the grade six classroom, a child came behind me and covered my eyes. I had no idea who it was. I was just getting to know the children. But nothing prepared me for who I was about to see. "Auntie Marci, its Jay" the child said. "Do you teach here?" he asked. He obviously did not see the surprise look on my face. If Jay is here, then I will see Dane, I thought. I buried that aspect of my past.

I went to my class with Jay following me babbling on about his mother and grandmother. I wished I had a padlock to close his mouth. From that day, Jay made it his duty for me to see him. He told me his two younger brothers were also here, Killian and David. I knew Killian but David I wanted to see.

Couple mornings after I got my wish, there was Cher, holding David's hand. She didn't see me and I didn't want her to. My heart melted when I saw David. I waited until break time then I went to his class and took him in my arms and held him tight. I looked at him and he smiled. He was adorable, he resembled both parents. I said to myself, so this was how my baby would look.

After this, David and I had a secret friendship. Every morning and evening, I would go to his class and hugged and kissed him. As he saw me he would ran into my arms. Because of this, so did all the other children. The two teachers teased me telling me to get my own. I would smile. I was very close to getting my own. The school year came and went and I resigned. I was asked to reconsider by the School Board and parents so I decided to do one more year as I had things in my life to sort out. I had mortgages to pay, two cars to maintain and I was also pursuing a Master's Program. Financially, it was not a good time to launch out. I also broke off my engagement to my boyfriend who tried to control me. That was just not me. I rented one of my houses, rented out both cars, my grandmother became sick and so I took on the responsibility of caring for her.

When I saw Dane face to face, I had mixed emotions. He never realized. A part of me wanted to strangle him and another part wanted to hug him. We talked on and off, the truth was, I tried to avoid Dane. My past had caught up with me and having Dane and David was a lot for me. David reminded me of what I left behind and Dane, the man who never realized he planted a seed somewhere. Dane however, was hard to ignore and pretty soon we started to chit chat often. It wasn't long that he started to be himself and chat me up. I asked him for Cher, he said they were not together and she went away. Here we go again, I thought, but I refused to go down that road again.

Killian kept getting into trouble and so he was sent to the Principal's office quite often. His mother leaving affected him. I decided to take him personally in my care. I didn't do this for Cher or Dane but out of my natural love for children. I started to look out for Killian and David just as I did with so many of the other children. Because of the children, Dane and I got to talk more often. He was involved in the football program. The children also seemed to gravitate towards him. I started looking forward to seeing Dane, he made my evenings. He would tease me and say "marry me." I was fascinated with Dane, he made me smile. I liked the way his eyes twinkle, how his nose twitched and his thin lips 'ah' he made me feel warm.

When Dane didn't pick up the children, I would miss him. I wasn't expecting anything from Dane, but it was the first for a while that someone made me tingle. It was funny how my life seemed to be going around in circles because here was Dane again in my life with sunshine. While talking one night on the phone, I told Dane about the abortion. He said he felt I resented him for something. The next day he saw me, he said he felt guilty. But I felt light as if I was released from a cage. If I were a bird I would have soared.

Dane used to travel often to buy equipment because he now had his own business. The last time he went away, I found myself missing him a lot. I could hardly wait for him to return. I had a lot that I wanted to share. I had started to open up and talk to Dane about so many things, something I had not done for quite awhile because I was very private and kept my personal life to myself. Dane stayed over for two days in Miami. The children went home early the Friday evening because Killian had a swollen ankle. When I went home, there was a message on the machine from Dane. It said, "Your husband called." I smiled; he made me do that a lot. You just can't take him seriously. At school, every time he saw me he would say "kiss me" and of course I just smiled.

Dane called me in the night and we spoke at length talking about school and his trip. There was a track meet the following day and I was going to help out but only because Dane would be there for me to talk to. I tend to ignore some of the parents, they had the wrong attitude. Dane called me the next morning and told me he was going to the airport to collect his luggage which was detained. A girlfriend was going to pick me up but I decided to go with Dane. He took sometime to pick me up so I decided to do a few things while waiting on him. One of them was warming up the car battery. This was one of the cars I had rented. It was rented to Mr. Isaac, the principal of Victoria Academy. My girlfriend was seeing him at the time so I rented him the car through her. He was in New York visiting her so I kept the car because his wife threatened to smash it. He was going through a bitter divorce and his wife resented the person he was seeing. Actually, that's why my girlfriend went away. I picked up the car from school because I had to protect my interest. Their affairs did not concern me.

I started to turn over the car engine because the car had been parked all week. I never normally drive the car. At the end of the agreement, I intend to sell both cars. While coming out of the car, Dane came. One of his workers drove. I got out the car and ran upstairs to get my bag. When I got back and went in the van, he asked me what Mr. Isaac's car was doing at my apartment. I explained to him. Nothing could have prepared me for Dane's reaction. Expletives were hurled at me, he accused me of being the principal's mistress, ooh that hurt. The more I tried to explain myself, the more he cursed me, the twinkle in his eyes were replaced by fire. I am almost sure if I looked hard enough, I would have seen smoke coming out of his ears and nose. This continued all the way to the airport. I could not believe this was the man who claimed he liked me. At first, I was amused but then I got angry. I was very good at holding my temper, so I rarely got angry because I did not like the feeling of anger. Dane said a lot of things which really hurt my feelings. I didn't go to the meet, instead, I asked him to drop me off at dancing. I could not explain how I was feeling. The thing was, Dane was not even listening, he was beyond reasoning. Moreover, he showed me no respect in front of his worker.

I went home and called Dane the night, but it made no difference, only that he wasn't using expletives. Nothing I said could convince him I wasn't seeing the principal. There went my weekend. The next day was Killian's birthday, of course I would not go to his party, not with Dane in that mood. I take very good hints at rejection. The next day at school, Dane barely spoke to me. He gave me two pens he brought. He refused to speak to me and I decided to leave him alone. I put the pens in a draw because I didn't intend to use them. The next two weeks of school, Dane avoided me and I kept out of his way.

By this, I was quite annoyed because I let him get under my skin, also because he was acting silly. One day, I looked out my class room and saw him and at that point, I wished I had a brick to throw on him or a big truck to run over him. I laughed at my thoughts. The truth was I like Dane in a different way. It wasn't that I wanted anything from him or a relationship, but I had a connection to him and friendship was enough. I still looked after Dane's children because I cared so deeply.

This I was grateful for that at least he did not tell the children to stop coming to me. He never came to my classroom again so I made sure in the evenings the children waited for him outside.

School gave Easter Holidays and I wrote Dane a very long letter. I had to get it all out. If he didn't want to speak to me after, fine but I must be given the chance to express myself. I left the letter beside Killian's present. When I reached home I called the secretary and told her to deliver both packages personally to Mr. Dane because I fear of some student stealing the present and the letter getting into the wrong hands.

I went to Cayman for three days to promote my up coming business and also to cool out. When I came back to Jamaica, I then went off to the country for a seminar involving my studies.

I returned to school three days after it reopened. I did not want to go back and I had no desire. It was not just because of Dane, but I was anxious to get things done the way I wanted. Victoria Academy was a good school but the management were fanatics. They made Christianity look burdensome and did not practice what they put on paper. I went to my class with a heavy heart. It was strange because I was thinking of Dane and how much I missed his twinkling eyes. When I looked up and found myself staring in them, I was shocked, I looked behind me surely, he did not come to see me. I told him, "Whatever it is, I didn't do or say it." "Relax" he said,
"I am just saying hi." I didn't listen to the weather report a storm must be coming. I then realized that Mr. Isaacs must have said something to him though I didn't ask him to. I was glad to see Dane. I watched him leave as he reminded me of the Pillsbury toast man. Oh, how I wanted to squeeze him, I just wish he didn't have that effect on me. I smiled.

I was interrupted by the children's voice, "Miss, the bus is here." I looked up to see the bus turning. The children all ran to get their bags.

Dane and I started renewing our friendship. My grandmother died shortly after and one day, he touched my nose and said it was inevitable that we came into each other's lives. I think he is right but in a different way.

I looked at David in my arms. I felt healed, I felt light. Of all the treasures in the world there is nothing more precious than giving someone a piece of your heart. Dane doesn't really know it, but he and David have a special place in my heart.

I kissed David in the middle of his forehead and whispered, "I love you from the depth of my soul." He seemed to smile in his sleep. As the children all ran towards the bus, I lifted David in my arms and followed. I thought to myself maybe just maybe one day, I will tell him or my children this story. I looked towards heaven and smiled.
"It was inevitable."

That Old House

It was Christmas Eve 1992; it was quite different for my family. We were going to spend this holiday season apart.

Through a family crisis, we had been kicked out of our home which we have been living for the past twenty years. My uncle had thrown us out. My name is Marie and this is my story.

I grew up with the Morais family, Mrs. Morais had eight children as far back as my memories take me they are of Portmore. We moved from Vineyard Town to Edgewater. The house belong to Dobby Dobson, mama's first child. I don't know what was the arrangement at the time, I thought he had given her the house. I was only eight at the time but I remembered that house it was a beauty to behold, wall to wall carpet brick decoration, hanging chandeliers, WOW! The yard was quite big. I was excited because at the time Portmore was a new and upcoming community. Edgewater was one of the better schemes built by Matalon. When I was small, Portmore seemed far. I remembered taking the Jolly Bus which ride seemed to go on and on. I used to have to get up at six and walked to Bayside with Yasmin to catch the first J.O.S Bus. Those days the mornings were dark but some how the morning walks were fun.

The first people we met were the Chows, we have been inseperable since. Mrs. Chow had four children, Tanya the youngest went to school with Andre who was Dobby's son. From ever since Andre and I were allies. We kept each others secrets. According to family, history had repeated itself. Both our parents had also grown up together. So much for family, what was certain was that we both suffered emotionally from not having our parents around. However, we handled it differently. Andre spent a lot of time with Mr. Henry next door who he looked up to. Mark, his son, became Andre's friend.

45 North Edgewater has a lot of memories. In the beginning we all lived together, how on earth did we all ever hold under one roof. But those were the days of fun. I remember playing doll house until all hours. Amanda, Lisa and Shelly we took this thing serious. Mrs. Chow use to be at the house talking to mama until day light. This I enjoyed because it gave me an excuse to be on the street. Everybody knew everyone. There was Nursie across the road with her dogs. Drunken Pickersville in front of us. Mrs. Green's shop was down the road. Her daughters and I were friends. As to me, I knew everybody. l. Her car a VW Bug use to take us everywhere. Its name was "Hopie Goodness." Donna was the first to leave, she got married and migrated. After Donna then went Bunny. We had a lot of fun back in those days. Gary and Andrew use to dress up and fool Mabel. She would take her stick and hit them or she was always saying someone was stealing her milk and sugar. Then there was the other side where she always wanted to go on the street, once Gary locked the gate and Mabel jumped it and we all had to run after her.

Tony alias 'Fruitpunch' or Lionsshare' was my other idol, to this day Tony is still my favourite. You see he was the family clown and he always gave me money so I was always doing jobs for him, when we where kicked out I lived with him for a year. He was the next one to move. Andrew, Dobby's eldest son migrated. Gary went off to University.

There was a time in my life when I admired Gary; he gave me a push start in my studies. He used to study for hours and I actually imitated him for a while until I developed my own style. Gary was Mr. Fix it. He fixed everything around the house and he would paint it also. One summer, he decided to play school at least that was how I saw it. He gave Andre and me countless Maths to do from morning until night. Now I wondered what happen to this brother not because he liked Math so should the whole world and there began my hatred for the subject, to make matters worse I refused one day to do any work and I did get a fine beating. Well, from that day on Garfield Morais and I were no longer family, in my heart I called down brimstone and fire on him. Andre decided to comply because he didn't want any beating, can't say I blame him because with his 'red' skin it would show for days.But it's all good now

By this time the house became empty, it was Yasmin, Micheal, Andre, Mama and myself. Yasmin has and still is my all time favourite. That girl has been there for me and there isn't nothing I wouldn't do for her. Talk about imitating Yasmin had a zest I liked and so in terms of studying I kept right behind her she was always studying and so was I. But I learnt something early, education was the only way up. There was Micheal but he was different and I couldn't bother to figure him out. We had run ins but I mostly kept out of his way.

Then came the grandchildren, of course I became the official baby sitter. I actually enjoyed it. It was then and there I knew I had to do something involving kids. Francine was the first, I never forgot one summer spending time with uncle Bunny and looking after Francine and burning Angella's good sheet, heaven helped me. Well, I decided to hide the thing. Now how was I to know in my twelve year old mind this woman had such good nose, so I had to confess, Angella was not amused neither was I. Then came Jason, Emile, Alain, Romain, Sheldon, Xavier. The house use to be full of boys and of course, I enjoyed keeping them under manners, I was always called upon to baby-sit one of them, sometimes I was not in the mood, but most times I like having them. Jason, Emile and Alain and Romain became my all time favourite nephews, I tell you why. Jason and Emile lived with us. I took them to dentist, out, you name it. When Jason started school I took him. He used to be behind me everywhere I go. He used to have bad asthma attacks and I remembered rushing to the hospitals in the middle of the night. I recall spending my summers babysitting. Once Jason ran threw the glass door, my heart was in my mouth and he almost cut off his finger. Emile was a miserable baby once he was up you had better had his bottle ready.

There was a man who lived on the road his name was Mr. Levy. He used to give mama a ride. Emile would not stop calling this man "Big Head" all we tried to get him to stop as soon as Mr. Levy drove up he would say 'Hi Mr. Bighead.'

Well, I tell you 45 North Edgewater has been quite special to me, I remember the games I used to play in that house, once the fridge caught a fire and Andre and I tried to out it with water, we did get the shock of our lives. Then there was the time when a thief broke in, he didn't get any thing. Another time a thief tried to strangle me. Through hurricane Gilbert, we ate lots of corn beef and ran down water trucks. There were a lot joys, trials, failures, victory, sorrow, triumphs all born in that house.

I passed my exams in that house; I started college in that house. I had some good times from doll house to parties. I remember once mama gave me her partner money to give Mrs. Chow well, she had some bad dogs. I called but no body came. Then I saw Jeannette. She said let's use the money she would get it back and no one would know. The thing is, when you are a child, how stupid and naïve you are. I forgot about the money. Mrs. Chow asked mama, I had to go without lunch money for a week and Jeannette did not pay it back. I learnt a valuable lesson never let friends talk you in doing wrong things; nine out of ten times you are left to face it alone.

Yep that old house helped to form a big part of my character. Summer days were fun, hanging out with friends. I met Karen while living at 45. Christmas was okay, it was the time when mama got to see all her children at least those who were in Jamaica. Well, summer 92 Dobby Dobson rode into town after not hearing from him for many years and by the end of summer we were on the street so to speak. It happened so fast I really thought for a while that I was dreaming. No, No it was the real thing. The man said "Get Out" no explanation, nothing, at least I didn't get any. I mean these things happened to other people not us. While I could understand kicking us out, especially Andre and myself because from the man came we have been giving him "Hell." I had my reasons I don't know what was Andre's. But you kicked out your own mother, right then I made a vow, children were the last thing in my life, you give them your life and what do they do, stab you in the heart. It pained my heart to leave that house but I told myself I am going to work and buy mama a house I also at the time reaked Brim stone and fire on Dobby, those were my rebellious years.

I am now at peace with my self. All things have to come to an end, the "world is a stage, we must all play our part and then come off." No one knows why people do the things they do. That's something I told myself, I have no expectation of people and I don't expect anything from them. And so we moved on I would bet everyone would have their own stories to tell. 45 North Edgewater formed a very important part of my life. Every time I passed that old house it always bring back memories.

The Power of the P- - sy

Women have been long known for their sexual manipulation and dominance. However, some women have not learned how to tap into this unique resource. The women who have harness this power have benefited from it in many ways.

What is it about what a woman holds between her legs? It has driven many men insane, some have taken their own lives, others want to control it and many want to taste it. A woman's p- - sy is mystical and it is the driving force behind many women. They use it to control their men and command what they want. Any woman who is in tune with her sexual desires knows from meeting a man if she is going to sleep with him or play with him.

From ancient times women have been using their p- - sy to control men. It knows no boundaries and according to Shabba Ranks "it can't done". David in the Bible sent his soldier to war to get his wife. Samson told Delilah his secret and was defeated. Oh the charm of a woman. I read a slogan once that said "Once you have a p- - sy you will never be broke". Let's analyse this carefully. Many persons will say this is vulgar but it is reality. I am not talking about prostitution here.

How many women have slept their way to the top of the corporate ladder? Others have married not for love but for financial security. Many men have called themselves player. But the recipients (the women) will tell you otherwise because these women have gotten houses, cars, expensive gifts and an education out of these men. The Power of the P- - sy.

P- - sy talks and talk it does. You would be surprise how a woman use her groin to mesmerize a man that someway, somehow he just can't seem to walk away. You are going to say this is not all there is to life and that is true. But the reality is that it happens. "The Slam" "Hot Wuk" "Back it up" is all real. Women who have learnt to use their P- - sy and make it work for them. There is nothing vulgar about it. You would be surprise to see the women who exploit their femininess. The professional, the pretty girl, the educated woman, the simple house wife, they come in all shape, looks and sizes.

Readers some of you maybe thinking how "lewd" this is but others will be shaking their heads in agreement. Because you have either seen it or done it. I read a cartoon that showed a little boy and girl. The little boy told the girl he had two marbles, she told him she had five. Frustrated he told her he had four sweets, she told him she had ten. He then pulled down his pants and pointed to his penis, he told her, "I know you don't have any of this." "True" she said. But she pulled up her dress and pointed to her vagina and told him, "With one of this, I can have as many of those.

As comical as this seems, it is a mystery that holds true. Society has found many ways to curb women by stating that you can't do what the guys do and still be a lady. What utter nonsense. All of this is just a way of men protecting their egos because they can't take what they give. Some women have bought into being the perfect lady and we definitely welcome this. After all God forbid we wouldn't want all women to be flaunting their greatest asset. I can't imagine what this world would be like.

To the readers of this excerpt, whether you agree or disagree, finds this eerie outrageous or to be true, the fact remains that the Power of P - - sy is real and very much alive in our world. Women who have mastered the art of charm and their sexuality find themselves in comfortable positions. Please note that I am not stating that women should and do sleep around to get what they want. I am merely making the point that in our present world, sex is a symbol and sells any and everything.

All I am saying is that many women have bought into this and see no problem in using their natural resources to get what they want. Whether we want to believe it or not, it has work for many women. *The Power of the 'P.'*

Two Nights of Passion

I don't know which was worse, the beads of water that formed perspiration on my forehead or the voice on the other end of the phone that sent chills down my spine, which went down to the sole of my feet.

My thoughts went down memory lane. I remembered that first time I saw this figure coming up my walkway I said to myself, how handsome. He was of brown complexion, tall and lean. His body was quite athletic looking. He had a butt which I fell in love with, God he was good looking.

But there was a problem, he liked my friend Lecia. However it turned out that Lecia who was very good at fooling men was not the least bit interested. I couldn't imagine why. We went out quite a lot and I saw him a few times and we became close.

One night he came and picked me up and we went back to his house. He looked so desirable. I sat on his bed and we started talking. The next thing I knew he was kissing my legs, it did feel good but there was a problem. It was my time of the month and I was feeling terrible cramps, his lips kept going, it was so good but I would have preferred a good massage. I couldn't stand it any longer the pain was getting worse. I stopped him. He drove me home in silence. I never saw or heard from him again. So much for that.

It has been one year and some months since I had seen Calvin, so much happened since then. My mom died and I was in final year at University. I searched relentlessly for his number and when I found it excitement jerked my entire body. We chatted about the past, present and future. The next time I called he said, "Why don't you come over." My bones jerked. You don't know how I longed to hear him say that. I gave him the directions of where I was. I was so anxious to see him.

Calvin had changed. He drove a different car and now he wore glasses, nevertheless, he was still quite sexy. When we reached his house, he went to lie down; of course I was doing all the talking. He pulled me beside him and touched me. I asked him if he touched every girl that came to his house. That made him freeze so I kissed him. He then touched me on my breast that sent off fireworks in my body. He then trailed his tongue along my neck that was it, I wanted him and I was not going to let him get by me. He then took off my shorts, then came my panty and T. shirt. When he took off his clothes, I was amazed his body looked even better without clothes. He kissed me all over by this time I really wanted him. It hurt so badly but I wanted it, in fact, I needed him. I parted my legs I had to have him.

My heart was beating so fast when his tongue met my tongue. I took it hungrily. I begged him to come because I couldn't stand the pain. He adhered to my wishes then we had a shower together and his lean body against mine felt good. I put on back my clothes and by this, my womanhood was aching with pain.

Calvin wanted me again I wanted him too but the pain was scorching as if I had been burnt. I refused him and so he took me home. We drove in silence and I had to beg him to follow me to my door. He had detached himself. He kissed me goodbye, it was a quick one as if he was hurrying to get rid of me. Then he was gone.

I know that I had been used. And so it was, be never called. I was the one who kept calling. I could always hear the urgency in his voice to always get rid of me. But I kept hoping he would first like me. I asked him how come he never called me back, he barely wanted to answer. My aunt and uncle laughed me to scorn, it was obvious I cared about someone who couldn't care less if I exist. How could I have been so careless? But I couldn't go on beating myself because I allowed it. From the beginning I knew I was fooling myself. Sex is not love and we can't let our hearts and bodies rule our mind and soul.

I watched the rain beating from the roof top falling on the leaves, washing them, giving them a new look, fresh start. Tomorrow is another day and I believe my experience has taught me a lesson.

Bang! Bang! Bang!

That's the sound of gunshots flying past my window. My lights are out the house is still. I am crouch down in my cupboard. I close my eyes and imagine myself to be somewhere else. I live in East Kingston a PNP stronghold. The sound of gunshots was normal. I grew up hearing them and chances are I may die by them.

I am a domestic helper and I work in Cherry Gardens. I love my employers; it is like they have been God sent in my life. I have two children a boy and a girl. It is very hard. I am a single parent and I did not complete high school but I was determine to give my children an education. "Bang!" the shots continued.

I refused to allow my children to continue in this cycle of violence and of poverty. Girls started have children from the age of twelve. Young boys succumb to gangs. Few persons got out of this life of squalor and crime. No one cared, not politicians, not the media, not uptown Jamaica, and certainly not the police force.

When I became pregnant, my children's father walked out. I was young and ignorant. He was older, I was still a child. But I had no guidance. I mistook sex for love. "Ghetto life is serious." There is no one to hold your hand when all you see around you is crime, sex, drugs and injustice. You start to believe that's all there is to life. I had my first child at fourteen by nineteen I had the second and their father walked out on me. He wanted to abuse me physically and I told him not in this life.

I knew there had to be more to life. I had my tubes tied and I did days work to send my children to school. I had to have better for my children. My mother had ran off to the United States and my father I have never seen. My grandmother tried but poor woman she was tired. My children were not going to be a burden. I had to have better for my daughter and son.

"Whoosh!" a fire bomb flew past my window shining light inside. 'Thud!' it landed but seems to have outed. "All f- - - labourite fi dead" came the voices outside. Screaming is heard in the distance. I was alone at home. I thought to myself how frightened my grandmother would have been. She passed a year earlier. God bless her.

In the beginning it was extremely difficult to provide for my children but I stuck it out. I took them to school and I picked them up. I went to Jamal classes and learned to read. I felt so proud. I could read with my children. My life changed when a friend of mine introduced me to a family who was looking for a helper. The Lees were honest and genuine people. They had three children, two boys and one girl. I was taken into their lovely house and showed kindness.

They paid me above minimum wage and gave me encouragement. I never allowed my children to go home by themselves, I would pick them up or have a neighbour whose children attended the same school pick them up for me.

My children were not allowed on the streets or anywhere without me. I did not want to lose them to the streets. I bought them a lot of books and on Saturdays I would take them to the library. My son was the older and I told him to look out for his sister. We only had each other.

My employers took an interest in my children. When the violence flared up, they made us sleep at their house in a back bedroom. They bought them games and clothes and would buy them or included them in any activity their children were doing. For this, I have been grateful. My children learnt to swim among other things. They were able to go to good high schools. My son went to Kingston College and my daughter goes to St. Andrew High School. I save and I threw partner. I am hoping to buy a house.

My son is now at University studying in Natural Science and he lives at my employers as their daughter is also at University. My daughter also lives with them. This has taken a huge burden off me. I can never repay these people. Because of them, my children are getting an opportunity to rise up out of their circumstance. I tell my son when he starts working he will have to help me with my daughter's university fees. I would also like to go back to school myself and pursue my dream of becoming a nurse.

I look around me in my community and see the poverty and the hopelessness. The crime and the squalor, even animals' live better. There seem to be no change. The year rolls on and things get from bad to worse. The little boys grow up to be gunmen or they are killed before turning sixteen. Despite these circumstances, women keep having more children which fuel the cycle.

I look up and realize that morning was on the horizon. I heard angry voices and police siren. It is the same story all over. The police and residents in a battle as to who shot who or who was wrong or right, I never get involved. I use the excuse of having a live in job. I scurry around to pack a few things to take to work. I check in once in a while on my house. My neighbours keep an eye for me. I can't wait to move out of this area.

No one knows of my plans except my employers. I dare not tell anyone. I am planning to buy a two bedroom apartment for my children and I. When I leave, I plan to leave everything behind. The house I will give to someone who wants it and everything inside. It belonged to my grandmother. I want nothing to remind me of East Kingston except my memories.

I look forward to this day with great anticipation.

Hurricane Dean

There it came out of nowhere. Like a vulture ravaging its victims. Dean came packing winds, taking roofs and flooding houses. It was on a war path, it was not partial whose house it visited, rich, poor, rural, white, black or brown. Dean was here
to show who run things. Not dons, politicians or gangs, but Mother Nature.

Oh yes, every now and then all around the world man must be humbled in being reminded that he really is not in charge. This reminder comes in the form of earthquakes, hurricanes, storms, tsunami etc. Oh how small man is when it comes to the wake of natural disasters.

I sat inside listening to Dean rant and rave bellowing at person's doors to be let in. When they refuse, he tried to lure persons to come outside appealing to their curiousity. When Dean huffed and puffed and could not blow person's doors down, it took off their roofs, or sent objects through windows. He was out for destruction, light posts were sent to the ground, and trees were sent flying. Cars slammed in walls, the sea returned to claim back its course, taking people houses with it.

Oh, what a hurricane! Having lashed the island, Dean slowly moved away on August 19, 2007. It went in search of its next victim. The aftermath was devastating. Some people lost their homes, lives, and all their possession. People are left to pick up the pieces and move on. The rebuilding process has begun. For many, it will take sometime. For others, Dean has broken their spirits how many times must they rebuild.

Hurricane Dean has left laughing at the legacy it has left behind the tragedy, the discomfort, the unemployment. Dean is victorious it has dethrone Gilbert and it has made Ivan seemed tiny in comparison to its onslaught. It's been a nightmare for many persons. There is a saying "this too will pass." Dean has passed but the memories will remain for many years to come.

I Am Who I Am

As for back as I can remember about my life, I have always been different. I was never your regular girl. I always had my own style of doing things.

One of the things that happen to women is that society puts us in a straight jacket. You should dress a certain way, or look a certain way, and if you are single and over thirty, then it's a problem.

I made a decision in my life at an early age that I would not live by society's expectations. I would not be stereotyped of how a woman should look or behave. I was going to do what pleased me. This was why education was important to me. I truly believed that having a solid education would enable me to become independent.

"I am who I am and who I am needs no excuses". What you see is what you get. Far too many women are living their life for somebody. As women, we have to get a grip of ourselves. I have often said that it is important to have a sense of self because when you do, society nor anyone can change who you are or what you believe in.

Far too many women suffer from low self esteem. They strive for something that does not exist. They think if they wear brand name or have expensive things it makes them somebody. They strive to look and live as Halle Berry, Beyonce etc. But trust me, celebrities have their own demons to battle.

Too many women feel they have to be in a relationship to the point that they stay in abusive relationships for the fear of being alone or not being financially independent. I keep asking the question, what is being alone? Because I have met quite a few women in relationships that are very lonely. Women must break the cycle of letting society put them in a box of how they should look and dress. Women need to stop let men decide who they are. We were not put on earth to serve men. (Please note I am not bashing men). Each woman is created as an individual with unique attributes.
You do not need someone or a man to validate you.

I say to all women, love yourself. So what if you are not perfect, no one is. There will always be someone greater and lesser than you. Highlight the wonderful things about you and use that to enhance your life. Work on the negatives but celebrate you. Love the skin you are in. So what if you think it is not perfect, if there are ways you can work to improve it, by all means do so but know that you are beautiful in every single way. Any one who doesn't like it does not deserve to be in your life.

I told myself as a woman that I would not settle with an unfulfilled life. I would live life to the fullest, pursue all my dreams whether I fail or succeed. I would not settle to have a man in my life just for the sake of being in a relationship. No way.

It took a special man to love me and if it's not what I want then I prefer to be single.
I was not going to live a basic life of trying to make ends meet or trying to wear the latest fads to keep up with others.

I was not going to be kept down because of my colour. Women wherever you are 'Be strong.' It doesn't define you and do not let anyone tell you otherwise. I have had people telling me I was strange and not normal. But I never listened; it went through one ear and came out the next.

If you are single, love it. If you do not have children, celebrate it. If you are married and with kids, you are an individual, live, love and be happy. Your life is what you make it. It is a myth that you need someone or something to complete you. Love the skin you are in. I know I do.

Deja-vu

Here I am alone in my world, tired and frustrated. My life seems to keep going around in circles. How do I break this cycle? I feel so alone, unloved, unwanted, misunderstood. For some strange reason I keep making the same mistakes over and over. I have no friends, lover or family. My so called friends keep using me, men always leave me.

I am asking myself, what is it that I keep doing wrong? Was I buying people? I really like to give and believe in the spirit. But what I am noticing is that I have people around me who are taking. They are not interested in me as a person, how I am or what I am going through. I have been spending a lot of time reflecting. During this time, I have come to the conclusion that I must change my life.

I became really ill and had to spend a great deal of time in bed. There was no one. I was all 'alone' where was everyone? I thought. I considered myself to be a caring, genuine persons yet no one was calling to see how I was feeling. My room was dark but most of all it felt lonely.

It appeared to me that I had no girlfriends. They were either married or had children. Their lives revolved around their children, spouses or jobs. Those with who I was in contact with, I had nothing in common. Our interests took us along different paths. I was not insecure, I was confident successful and beautiful. Yet, why was I so alone? I somehow had not realized this state of loneliness until I was alone in my darkness. It is amazing how sickness clears your mind and allows you time to think or how lying in one place for a long time gives you time to reflect.

Men I have become immune to. I had two serious relationships that didn't work out. After that, I have been in and out of relationships with married men, this I somehow can't seem to shake. These men are attracted to me as fly to garbage. Though each time I keep telling myself it's the last time, I will still enter into such relationship, it keeps repeating itself. The irony in all of this is that these relationships are usually very good. This makes it very hard to break away from. But I keep telling myself this is wrong, I do deserve more. But Daja-vu always gets in the way. I feel trapped in a pen like an animal.

Where and how did this all started? I wondered. I remember growing up as a teenager how I long for my mother's love. I did everything to please her. Yet she with held her love. It was only given to my other siblings. After a while, I gave up trying to please my mom. I became estranged to both my mom and my siblings. I really didn't care what they thought and I am no longer a part of their lives.

I refuse to believe that I was scarred in anyway or carried emotional baggage. But something deep inside me wanted to make sense of my life. How do I free my emotions? How do I stop the feeling of rejection that takes me over when it seems as if my friends or lovers do not return the love I extend to them?
Deja-vu seems to always be at my heals chasing me, haunting me.

My last lover I was so madly in love with. We shared many precious and intimate moments. Of course he wasn't mine, yet I truly loved him wholly. I tried hard not to fall for him, but my emotions as always gave in. Try as I may, I don't know how to give a portion of myself. In what ever I do I must give my all. Alas it is causing me a nervous breakdown.

I don't have any answers at this moment, but I know that I must rid myself of this demon that keeps haunting me, this parasite that keeps draining me. I must absolutely and entirely be strong. I will now close my eyes as the darkness enfolds me.

Letter to Dale

5 Angry Road
Disappointed P.O.
Broken Heart

Dear Dale,

I do not intend to be writing you or calling you every minute. I am still in shock. It's not that I had any expectation of you. I had no hopes of starting a relationship with you. After locking away myself for sometime, it was refreshing to talk with someone who made me laugh. I thought I could relate to you but I was wrong.

You have judged me, charged me and convicted me. The irony in all of this is my innocence. You once told me not to judge you. Why don't you practice what you preach? How did I let you get to me to cause me stress? You have upset my equilibrium; you have been a torn in my side.

I have never lied to you. But how many lies have you told me. I am single, are you? I doubt it. This has convinced me even more, that I am better off staying by myself. You have not even listened to me. I am not sleeping with my boss. I am not even attracted to the man. Is that so hard to comprehend? Do you sleep with all you female workers?

The person he is involved with and I are good friends and we all share a friendly relationship. You are telling me that I played you. Are you serious? Who played who? I am not some careless girl. I refuse to let you hurt me; I am not going there again.

You have disappointed me. I was beginning to like you AGAIN. You have proven to be an asshole. The thing is you lump all women as the same and I am not going to let you bring me down. I am not going to force you to believe me. To hell with what you think.

Dale, I got you out of my system before, and I will do it again. There is nothing that I want from you. But I wanted us to be friends. That is impossible because you think little of me, but I can see why. A wise person once said, "So a man is so he thinketh." Because of who you are, you think the same of every woman who enters your life. Not everyone wants to sleep with everyone they come in contact with.

I have a simple motto: Live Simple, Expect Little, Give Much. I have no expectations where people are concern. It makes life easier, but at the same time, you can't keep just walking away when people care for you. You are very good at that.

Dale, I hope at some point in your life you allow someone to love and care for you, and in return treat them good. You can't keep running and leaving behind a trail of pain. I will miss you. I thought we were similar.

I am saying this for the last time; I was not involved with my boss. You treated me disgracefully and unfairly. I have forgiven you, life is too short. "But I will never allow you to get close to me again."

Same person

The Day My Mother Died

The day my mother died I could not cry. There in the grave lay someone I didn't know. For who she was I had no idea. I remembered the last time I saw my mother she was laughing and in high spirit. Then out of the blue my aunt called me to say my mother had died. How? No one seems to know. I stood there amidst all these people but I was not apart of them. I had isolated myself from this family long ago.

There was my aunt Gem with her false self. She thought her children were better than my mother's. Yet her daughter sat beside her with a big tummy, and as if that wasn't bad enough, she went and got married to cover it up. My aunt was bragging to everybody about her daughter's rich husband. Please, the man was a druggist. I do not know who she was fooling. I found them totally amusing. My family was a sham.

I was tired of my family secrets and lies; I wanted to be far from them as possible, that I made sure of. Prior to my mother's funeral, I had not seen them in ages. I had even stopped listening to my mother's complaint by not visiting her for a while. She constantly complained about her family, yet she allowed them to continuously hurt her. I got tired of it.

But maybe it was my listening ear that kept her going. Now I even hated my family more. I had dreams for my mother. So many things I wanted to do for her. Buy her a house, give her a trip, nice clothes, so many dreams. It was just not fair. My mother worked so hard. She should be reaping her hard work. But where was she, six foot six.

What then does life have to offer? You work like a dog and then you die. Why bother? I have told myself I do not want children because they only make you poorer. I really do not care what everyone say or think of me. I refuse to live as how my mother lived, poor and hungry.

I watched them lower my mother's coffin in the earth. Soon she would be alone, transitioning into another life of loneliness. I do hope my mother was in heaven because she was such a good person. She often times was too good to the point where people exploited her goodness.

As everyone walked away, I stood there trying to savour the last few minutes with my mom. I whispered, "Mom I am sorry to have left you but I hope to see you some day."
When I looked around, I was alone. So called families and friends were gone. I know this was how the rest of my life was going to be. I had no intentions of going to any family gathering. I did not belong. I wanted to be alone with thoughts.

As I looked up to heaven, I thought to myself, "I am all by myself." The day my mother died I could not cry. I wish I did because maybe I would have felt better. I walked away from my mother's graveside feeling empty. I had lost something from my life that could never be replaced. On top of it all, I had no one. Bye mom.

TRIBUTE TO CAROL GOBERDON

She was always smiling
Her freckled face
Her exuberance personality
You were an angel
Childlike but not childish

DIAL-A-PRAYER

On and off all day I've tried
I can't get any answer.

Was I calling a wrong number?
Is he out?
I'll try once more-
check in the big book-
dial carefully.
A busy signal!
Could God have left his receiver off the hook?
(Someone's at the door. They'll have to wait).
Dial 112
"Operator-is this number still in service? Yes?"
Dial it again. And still no answer.
I'm positive my line's not out of order.
(Will that knocking never stop?)
His phone rings on.
Easy for him to say "Need help? Call on me any time!"
What if I can't get through?
What if he's gone?

Or could that knocking be Him
calling on me?

PORTMORE DEH PON TOP

Yes mi dear, Portmore a it these days
Every time you miss smaddy and you think dem dead or migrate
Where can u find them?
Portmore of course

One time Nobody wanted to live there
All you hear 'too much salt, the place soon sink, me not crossing that bridge.'
But from Greater Portmore build, half of Kingston missing.
Where it gone? Portmore!

Yes chile Portmore a it
Even the franchise join in
Mother's, Kentucky, Burger King and then came Mega Mart

I overheard two women talking:

Woman # 1 – So fren, long time no see. Weh u did deh?

Woman #2 – I live in Portmore.

Woman #1 – Deh so too far, but mi need some way fi rent.

Woman #2 – Well, next door mi empty and it going cheap.

Woman #1 – eeh really, well cheapness neva too far fi travel. Let's go.

Yes mi chile, Portmore a di lick. Everywhere you turn building a go up.
Matalon think him could keep the people down by giving them matches box to live
in.
Hey, just fi dat people add on sideways, backways, upways
and every way you can think of.

Where can you find the hottest spots? Only in Portmore.
Whether you want to hang out, chill out or hide out.
When half the people missing from Kingston, just check
Cactus, Laroose, Jewels, Hellshire, you name it, Portmore has it.
Soon to be second city, fifteenth parish.

Anyway, I talk too long, I a go home. Weh u sey, weh mi live?
Portmore of course!!

REFLECTION

Lately I have been reflecting on life a lot. You wonder what the purpose of living is ? For what really is Life? It is a cycle, you were born you die. Then what is the purpose? I look at some people and I wonder what is the reason for the facade.

The impression, the pretense to get caught up with money. Why, after all we really are here for just a time. I don't know it puzzles me. So many people are unhappy. They go through life pretending, trying to keep up with the Jones. Oh boy.

For me, all I ask God for is to be able to help people and for happiness, to be me at all times to be honest both with others and myself. Life is complicated but it's something you have to understand. We are only here for a time. Our attitude plays a major role.

If God grant that I live to ripe old age, I ask only for serenity and wisdom as each day goes by to grow graceful. Thank you Lord for opening my eyes, it is worse to have sight but lack vision. Where there is no vision, the people perish.

"A man who hears will increase learning "– Proverbs 10 vs. 1

The saddest thing in life is wasted talent. You just have to accept people for who and how they are.

People never really change

Life is too short to figure people out
Life is too short not to love
Life is too short to be caught up with what people
What can money buy?

"Money will buy:
A bed but not sleep
Books but not brains
Food but not appetite
Finery but not beauty
A house but not a home
Medicine but not health
Luxunes but not Culture
Amusement but not happiness
A crucifix but not a savior
A church pen but not heaven "
Why then do we get stressed out trying to aquire so many material objects? We cannot take them with us.

WE WERE CREATED

In his likeness, we were created
We are not perfect
God created the earth in six days
First there was darkness, then came light
On the seventh day, he rested.
First there was Adam, then came Eve.

Yes, we were created
Put on earth, to love, to procreate, to serve
We were created
In his image but not in his likeness or his ways
But we were created anyway.

SOMETIMES

Sometimes I sit alone at home
waiting for your calls
but only in anticipation, that's all.
Sometimes I wonder, what it would be like
you and me again.
But when I face reality and know we can only be
friends.

Sometimes I'm told you'll get over him, don't worry
but when I think of what we had, I can't
help but feel sorry.

Sometimes it is said, "Life goes on, carry your heart"
but then they didn't say what to do
if yours is totally split apart.
Sometimes I'm so lonely, so empty, so upset
but just thinking about the wonderful times I spent
with you.

Sometimes I want
Then sometimes I don't
I think
He'll call and something inside tells me "No he won't."

Sometimes I want you back more than
words can tell
but then life goes on
"So what the hell!"

CURSE

There I was amidst the crowd
People shouting, people laughing
Yet no one saw me, no one spoke to me.
My black face stood out in this place
Yet I was invincible.

Some people stared at me with
Strange expressions on their faces
Was it curiosity? Was it mockery?

The sun danced on my golden nappy hair
My black skin glistened from the
Oil I used
I weep silently. The colour of
My skin will always haunt me.

I AM NOT LOOKING

I am not looking, she says
Why bother, I don't want a man
I am not looking because men
are trouble, silly creatures
always horny, always perverted.

Why should I look, she says
for a man who will want me
to cook, clean, wash and perform
wifely duties.

No, I am not looking, so stop asking.

I HAD A DREAM

I had a dream last night
It was about a land I know
A beautiful place to be
No crime, no war, no drugs.
Our people loved each other
Each man his brother's keeper
Children respected their elders
Yes, a land where our people
were one
A land where our people were
discipline
Politicians were united, Whoops!
I had just awaken to hear the news
Playfair throat slashed
Man murdered on Waterloo Road
Then I realize it was just a
dream.
It was only in my dream.

TIME

Take time to love
Take time to dream
Take time to be happy
Take time to make friends
Take time to know God
Take time to pray
Take time to enjoy your life
Time is the healer of the soul
Take the time.

BEING BLACK

It's a trap to be black
I am black and hating every
minute of it.
It's a curse from God; It's
punishment.
Anything that was not good is
BLACK
Oh! How I hate being black
I am trapped in this colour
until I die · No way out
I will have to learn to live
with humiliation, ridicule, scorn.
Whosoever said black is beautiful
must have been mad – Mad I tell you.
Being black is a sin and a crime
Because I am black, I am looked down
upon, trampled all over.
Black is a trap so if you can avoid
being black, be white or brown
because if you are black
STEP BACK!!

WE ARE WOMEN

We are the women who have always been waiting.
Waiting on our men, hanging on to every word they say.
We are the women who bear our children and give them suck.
We are the women who sacrifice our lives for children, who fight through divorces,
who bring up our children alone.
We are the women who fought for our rights to be equal to our men.
We are the women who form the corner stone of every nation, who stand behind
our men.
We are the women who are always waiting, hoping, hanging on for security.
We are the women who grow old but strong.
We are the women who bear the world on our shoulders.
We are the women who are invincible, forgotten, and unheard of.

Yes! We are the women.

THERE RUNS A DREAM

There she stands in all splendor.
Luscious Psalms waving in the breeze.
Mouth watering coconuts on the coast
Beautiful people all smiling.
Out of many one people.
The sun shines brightly on her.
The rivers sing lustily in their cannels.
A blessed and devine country she is.
Beautiful Jamaica Oh! So fair

"Too rich to be poor."

IF ONLY

If only life was like a movie, with a well written script.
Good conquering evil and love prevailing in the end.
But then life would be all too boring.

If only troubles did not exist.
Wars were only rumours.
If only this was so, for…
Enemies should even have friends.
Friends should be forgiving.
But yet again there are unpardonable sins.

If only life was like a fairy tale.
If Only.

FORGIVE AND FORGET

How can I first forgive and forget, pretend as though nothing happened closed my eyes to reality and ignore morality?

How can I first forget what happened, as though you and I never cared? But I will not try for the impossible, regardless of my feelings and thoughts of you.

How can I be the same person again waiting for tomorrow to come with what may? As time is a healer of ills and ails that neither you nor I can erase.

If I had an eraser back then I would forgive and forget. As I erase the thoughts of you.
But I cannot clear the memories of my heart that trusted you.

THINKING OF YOU

When I think of you,
It makes me smile
When I remember your smile,
It makes me laugh
When I remember your laugh,
I close my eyes
When I close my eyes,
I see your face
When I see your face,
It makes me smile again.

GOD MUST HAVE KNOWN

God must have known why he made the sun, moon and stars
Why he created the earth and divided the valleys
God must have known why he made Adam first and then Eve
God must have known that a man would need a woman as a companion God must
have known why I was born
He must have known that this world would be an evil place to live
God must have known all these things, because He has never been wrong
God must have known

STILL - HE LOVES YOU

Sometimes in life it's hard to understand
Why it seems God isn't sending you a helping hand
Your burdens get heavier and seem to increase
And you find yourself praying for sweet release
You forget that joy is on the opposite side of sorrow
And you patiently wait to see what will happen tomorrow It is at times like these,
knowing that you are His daughter Gives you the confidence to have faith in His
character.

Sometimes it seems you can't understand His will
But because He loves you, you trust Him still
Knowing that He only wants what's best for you
And knowing too, that there's nothing else you can do
But believe that when you have no feet on which to stand He is gently holding you
in the palm of His hand
Caring and nurturing and protecting you too
Knowing you 'll love Him, no matter what He chooses to do.

God loves you; that, don't ever doubt
Even when He's whispering, though you want Him to shout God loves you,' don't
ever forget
That throughout your life He hasn't failed you yet
God loves you and He'll always be yours
Always with you through these endless hours
Remember, that God loves you and if at the start
You can't seem to trace His hand, just trust His heart.

AFTER A WHILE

After a while you learn the subtle difference
between holding a hand and chaining a soul.

And you learn that love doesn't mean leaning
And company doesn't mean security.

And you begin to learn that kisses aren't contracts and presents aren't promises.

And you begin to accept your defeats with your head up and your eyes open, with
the grace of an adult, not the grief of a child.

And you learn to build all your roads on today because tomorrow's ground is too
uncertain for plans.

After a while you learn that even sunshine burns if you get too much.

So plant your own garden and decorate your own soul, instead of waiting for
someone to bring you flowers.

And you learn that you really can endure...that you really are strong.

And you really do have worth.

IN THE WORLD OF PRETENSE

The rich - upper class - middle class
These who pretend, the have and have nots
It's all about pretense
Who has the latest God gets
Who just bought a new car, Camry, Honda, BMW
Cellular phones can be heard ringing
In this setting it's all about money
It's a competition who can out do the other
No one is genuine
Many dislike each other
But it's all about pretense
So pretend they must
It's a money thing
Who just travelled to Miami or New York
Whose dress or outfit costs thousands of dollars
They discuss each other
X's car is quite common
Jake just lost his job, I guess they will have to move
Now out of that big house
Amy married a doctor, I don't think she really loves him
It's all part of a social scene
Some fit in, some don't
Others try to fit in
The facade continues, false laugh
One wonders why go to all this hassle, the lies, the pretense just to belong
Is it worth it?
Is it?
-

LOST LOVE

Where have you been for this long time?
Twenty years of love and devotion bottled inside
Now before you answer the question
Here is what I hope you will say
"Waiting for you my love"
I might have now been a queen
If we had met sometime before
Happily I would relinquish my crown
For time spent by your side
To reincarnate my love
Hold my tongue and I will speak through my eyes
Block my ears and I will listen with my heart
If it had not been for you my love
The best parts of life, I would surely miss
But now I can boast of having my very own prince
Who is handsome, smart, loving, caring, a friend
With the name of??

PREGNANT WOMEN

You see them here, you see them there Tall and short, fat and slim
Up town, down town, all around town
Big breasts, fat bottoms, bent backs
Some big, some small
It is the same
"They are all pregnant"

You see them walking, driving or taking bus
Long hair, short hair,
Black or brown
Wobbling like a clown
Some wear rings, some have none
Some sad, some glad, some the men went on the run Whatever the state or
whatever the case
They all have one thing in common
They are, "PREGNANT WOMEN."

A BEATEN WOMAN

"Woman holds her head and cry"
This has become a ritual
He beats her once
Said it would never happen again
She forgives him - took him back
The beatings stopped, only for a while
But it started again
Once, twice, thrice
Now it is a part of her life
It comes with being a wife
Biff - if dinner is not cooked on time
Baff - she committed a crime by staying out late
But that was her fate
Everyone asked her why she stayed
She says she loves him, this is the only way
And so a punching bag she becomes
"Woman holds her head and cry."

STREET BOYS

There is a big rush to the car, we come up with nothing
People scorn us, they wind up their windows,
They see us coming but we are humans too
All we need is love.
It's a jungle out there, the bigger boys beat up the smaller ones and take away
what little money they get from motorists.
Some of us have no homes, no parents, no one.
"I have made no money today,"
What will I tell my mother?
I wish I could be a normal boy, with a home, mother,
father and a home cooked meal
All we need is love, yet society rejects us
We are dirty, we are poor, is it our fault?
To be poor is a crime, this is quite true
To be poor is to suffer, to live in anguish, squalor, dirt, but who cares,
Not the police, not society.
I have one suit of clothes, no shoes, no bed to rest my head
I don't know what it is to have
But who cares.?

ABORTION

A woman cannot never forget the children she got that she did not "get" Abortion
haunts you everyday
It is with you to stay
Every time she sees a baby her heart jumps
Her womb weeps for her dead child
No one understands the pain, the guilt she feels
It is hers alone to bear
She sees women with their babies
She hears their cries, the patter of little feet
Their happy faces
Her world is torn apart - a guilt she must bear all her life
A secret she has to keep to herself
A scar that cannot heal
She has died a thousand times
Abortion - will not let you forget the children you got that you did not get.

THINK POSITIVE

We can all achieve our heart's dreams and desires once we set our minds to it.
Always think positively, never allow yourself to be influenced or discourage by the
negative thoughts of others.
A healthy mind will ensure a healthy body and put you on the road to success.

LOVE

What really is love?
Is it when your heart beats fast?
Or when you get excited
Is love only for a time?
Does love passes?
Is it obsession?
Does it warms your heart and makes you feel as if you could burst?
Can love quickly turn to hate?
Love today hate tomorrow
Is it when you feel as if butterflies are in your stomach?
What then is love?
Love is not an emotion
Love is not jealousy, it is not unkind
Love is not felt in a single moment but rather comes with many years Love is
caring, to love is to know God
Love is through thick and thin
Love endures through sickness and health
Love is through good times and bad
Love cannot be bought
Love is not selfish
Love is a life long process, it redefines, it reshapes, it relives, it recreates It's from
the womb to the tomb
Love stands the test of time
Love is beautiful
Love comes from within

"HEART BRAKE"

Why me?
What have I done?
Except to have loved with all my heart
Now it's broken
Tell me
Was it your intention
To pretend you loved me
Then steal my heart and leave me lonely
Or was it a pure innocent mistake I had to bear
I know I will never love this way again
If loving someone is a crime
Then I am guilty
Let the sentenced be pass
But tell me one more thing
Was it a game to break my heart?
If so, you sure played it well from the start

THE FINAL FRONTIER

So much I have learnt in the ten years
So much had changed
Life - a gift from God
To what do we owe this life?
Why were we created?
As a matter of fact
We are really here just for a time
Only passing through
And then we are gone
God has put us here only for a time
We shall pass this way only once
So live your life to the fullest
Put God in the centre of your life
Dream your dreams
Love, laugh, share, and procreate!
Until you must join your saviour forever
So much I have learnt.

LONELINESS

I am surrounded by people yet I am all alone,
I see people's mouths moving yet I hear them not,
I feel lonely, my life seem empty,
I see people smiling, yet I can't feel them,
I see love being passed around, yet I can't get none,
I am lonely for I am misunderstood,
I am lonely for I am not loved,
I am lonely for I have been rejected,
I am in a family yet I am invincible,
Loneliness and I are friends, we are inseparable, Loneliness is it a state of mind?
Or is it reality?

BUS VIBES

You get to the bus stop very early
But that does not make a difference
You have to wait for at least four hours
Children chattering, people sweating
Sellers shouting, flies pitching
"Look out for the pick pockets"
The stench fills the air
Move out of the mad man's way
The sun delights itself on you
"Ha" the bus comes at last
The driver smirks - Good I have kept them waiting.

Everyone rushes to the bus
Biff! Bang! Bash
You need not try, if you cannot karate
The bus fills up quickly
People hanging off
Half the people outside
The bus is ready - it drives off
It is torture time again
Another three hours wait.

STREET PEOPLE

As I sit on this hard sidewalk begging, I am distracted by the beautiful building in front of me it stands tall and erect and it seems as if it reaches up to heaven. My eyes hurt from looking up. Its colours were purple and white with purple awnings at every' window overlooking the lawn.

The lawn was evergreen and immaculately clean. I got up from where I was sitting; it was as if some magnetic force was pulling me to this building. I was mesmerize and excited at the same time. As I came closer, I notice a swimming pool; I heard laughter no doubt people were having fun.

I smell something delicious being prepared, my stomach churned and my mouth watered, longing for food. I clutched to the fence wanting to belong to this scenery'. I noticed people in red uniforms, this I saw as danger.

The great monument in front of me was worth admiring, yet it held some mystic force that sent a message to you that only a certain class was allowed to enter its gates.

It was as if I was pushed back by an invisible force and so I kept my distance. With one last look I turned and head back for the streets.

FREEDOM

As I sit staring through the window reflecting on my past, oh! How I wish life was a book, where I could turn the leaf and start over again.

I looked at the children playing in the street, enjoying themselves, totally oblivious to the world around them. I wish I was like them but no, no I am trapped, yes trapped as a bull in a pen. I wonder when will I ever be free, free to laugh, to love to be myself, when? When?

I felt the breeze sending chills down my spine, which form ripples on my skin. It felt deliciously good. The trees dance in the wind and lifted their leaves proclaiming the breeze.

Oh! How I wish I was free and could grow wings and just fly, where to? no specific destination.

Here I am instead tied down no friends, no money, no man, no mother, no love, no family, but I have instead five hungry children to feed, yet all I can do is look through the window.

For it is only then I feel free, yes free.

I felt someone tugging at my dress and realized it is my youngest child. Pitiful eyes staring at me pierce my very soul.

I am back to reality back in my cage again, back to slavery, subject to work. When will it end? When!

I closed the window tomorrow again I shall escape and feel FREE.!

Nostalgia

I was deep in thought as I was waiting for Mannon to join me for lunch. Just calling his name made me wet. Mannon and I have known each other for ten years. He is twelve years older than I. Mannon, even though he doesn't realise it, taught me a lot about life, work and people. I still remember how we met. Somehow that day has always been fresh in my mind. I had gone to our neighborhood grocery shop for my mother. I was quite upset because she was always sending me to the shop. "Why can't she just decide what she wanted once and for all?" I thought to myself.

Mrs. Gray's shop had been pack as usual and this made me twice upset.
Mrs. Gray's shop has been around for as long as I can remember. I grew up with her children and she used to take me to school. I always thought her to be quite miserable, nevertheless, I had a lot of respect for her. People frequented the shop for various reasons, some to buy grocery, drink, rum, or just to hang out.

I came up in the midst of a discussion and I quickly became part of the discussion. Even though I was only eighteen years old, I was quite mature beyond my years or so I had been told. I could hold my own in any discussion. However, there was this young man telling me how much I was pretending to be big and of course, I was not amused. But it was my look. It always gave me away to lead people into thinking I was much younger than I looked.

When we were through buying we began talking to each other and somehow I felt as if I had known this young man for quite a while. I even found myself following him home and this was quite unlike me. My mother must be swearing by now I thought to myself, but I didn't care. I wanted to know more about this man. I found out his name was Mannon, and he didn't live far from Mrs. Gray's shop. I knew his house but I never noticed him over there before. We chatted as if we have been old friends for years. Mannon and I were born on the same month and only a day apart. He was born on November twelfth and I on the thirteenth.

Mannon took me home and we exchanged numbers. We became instant friends. Since then we were inseparable. I would always be at Mannon's house. He lived alone and I liked that. He was always telling me about his family or playing music for me. Truth is, I had a secret crush on Mannon, but somehow I felt he just saw me as his little sister. Also he had a girlfriend who was two years older than me.

The more I saw Mannon, the more I fell in love with him and he didn't even have the slightest clue. We enjoyed each other's company. He would take me all over the place with him, to his brother's and sister's house, even to his girlfriend's house. We would spend hours at his house talking in the darkness or running jokes.

He asked me once if I was a virgin and I said yes. He laughed at me and I felt hurt because I never could understand what he found so funny.

Certainly Mannon was clueless of my passion for him. When he touched me he sent fire through my body. Thinking of him made my nipples erect. I could not quite imagine how he had such a hold over me. When he whispered in my ear, I always wet myself. He had an overwhelming personality which some would find intimidating but quite the contrary, I found it a turn on. I would challenge his authoritative personality. I was always searching through or troubling his things and he would order me to stop, much to my delight in that voice which just turned me on.

One night we seemed to have passed our usual conversation. We started out simply as playing ended up with Mannon beginning to caress me. Oh, how it felt good. He ran his tongue down my spine and legs. How I wanted him. I was wet and ready, but suddenly he jumped up and said, "Sara go home." At first I protested, but when Mannon gives you a certain tone, you don't argue. I couldn't go home, I was confused and all sorts of emotions stirred up inside me which I could not explain.

We drove in silence to a house where by cousin was but I just could not go home. When Mannon let me off I walked home five minutes after. I had to clear my head. I could not sleep. I kept replaying the scene in my head. For years we never mentioned what had happened that night. I was suddenly brought back to reality by the presence of a waiter who had a concerned look on his face. "Are you okay madam?" he asked. I suddenly realised that even though the restaurant had air conditioning, I was sweating profusely, not to mention the stream flowing between my legs. "Y y yes." I replied,
"I am okay." "Can I get you anything to drink, until your friend comes?" "Water will be fine." I said.

I was at the Gallery one of the finest most extravagant hotels in town. It was owned by a long time line of English family handed down from one generation to the next. I was early for lunch and besides, I did not mind waiting. My eyes met two Caucasian males across the room who seemed to be having a business discussion. They must have been staring at me for quite awhile. One winked at me. I gave them a weak smile and turned my head. Men found me incredibly attractive or so I have being told.. But I could not see it. According to an admirer I had sex appeal and charisma.

The next time I saw Mannon I had changed. He was engaged. He gave me a tour of the house, which he had just done additions to. I had just finished my first degree and by now was a radical. I had no interest in Mannon's house. I wanted to grab him and make love to him. I wanted to run my tongue all over his body. God forgive me I thought to myself, but I had changed from being a little girl to a young woman. I was in touch with my sexuality and by this I had lost my

virginity. It was nothing I had imagined. It was boring, and so I dumped the guy. Hell, I was just curious after my escapade with Mannon.
It wasn't the same.

I was brought up to believe that women had no say when it came to sex. My mother had told me it was only the man who was supposed to enjoy it. She said count to fifty and then it would be over. Nor should a lady approach a man if she liked him. She should wait on him to initiate the move. So I had waited and I lost Mannon but these were the 90's and I can just imagine how she would chastise me for the thoughts that I was thinking right now of Mannon. She would make me confess my sins to Father Berthram since she is catholic. Right now I didn't care; I wanted to hold on to Manon's manhood and part my legs and ask him in a very sexy voice if he wanted it.

But things and time changed. At university, you meet people all from different walks of life. In the 90"s women were more open about their sexuality and they are not afraid to express it. After Mannon got married somehow things changed between us. I couldn't put my hand on what it was. I figured he was just taking his marital vows serious. His wife and I became good friends before and after she had their first son. But Mannon and I nevertheless barely exchanged two words.

On numerous occasions while driving we would pass each other. Our relationship had changed and I just could not understand why. This went on for sometime until after the birth of his second child. I was at his house while everyone was inside. I decided to leave and he followed me to my car. He asked me what happened to us. After a lot of coaxing I opened up and told Mannon how I felt about him. It didn't matter now anyway. I was only to discover that Mannon had felt the same way too. How dizzy I became. After all these years and not one of us letting the other aware of it. How different things' could have been.

I was now pursuing a Ph.D. in psychology and Mannon was the head of a large Petroleum company. We are even closer. I am engaged to be married but our relationship has nothing to do with our spouses. Mannon is happily married. What Mannon and I shared is special, a history which maybe we can share with our offspring someday.

I caught a glimpse of Mannon heading towards me. This is a man who no matter how I try I just can't get over him. I could get used to being married to Mannon. How I would love to have him come home to me every night. To give him hot baths, to crawl into his lap and put my arms around him;
to give him massages when he is tired, to greet him at the door. I could go on and on but Mannon wasn't mine, how unfair life can be, I thought.

Mannon came up to me and kissed me and told me how attractive I was, which was something we both could not explain; just how comfortable and okay it felt to be together. I saw the two white men looking and I figured they thought I am with my man. That was just it, Mannon and I had something so special that no one could or had the right to intervene and nothing in the world would let me destroy that. I took my right foot out my shoe and rested it between Mannon's leg, followed by my left foot and I started playing with him.

We stared into each other's eyes and no words were needed. We had gotten used to talking without words. We weren't having an affair but what we had was deep and precious without the infiltration of sex. It was pure but not innocent. We both knew we wanted each other but somehow would never risk losing each other. Mannon is the man I never got. To Mannon, I am the woman he could have gotten.

Mannon and I are so much alike we just seem to be able to tune into each other's feelings and thinking. We are very close. Maybe it's our birth month, who knows. But we are more than just friends, something neither can explain. I never want to lose this or him. Even if he moved to Africa and I to Asia, unless its through death over which I have no control. I can never love another man as I love Mannon. I truly believe he is my soul mate and I love him exclusively and treasure what we share. I blow a kiss over to him and he smiles, another one of our languages. He made a mark in my heart never to be erased.

Women's Strife

Sisterhood, women power, independent woman, what does it all mean? Women are still not united. Men divide us, children manipulate us. The world sets one standard for men and another for women.

Women do everything but work together. They criticize each other. Men put them against each other. Many times women do not realize how silly this is. What goes around comes back. Why curse a woman over a man.

Women do not know what it is to have each other's back. They are the first to sell out each other or snitch on their girlfriend. Men do not do that, when they decide to stick together they mean it.

Corporate women when they decide to get dirty are dangerous. They will lie, cheat, gossip or sleep their way to the top of the ladder. There is no other species as manipulative as women. They will observe the situation and scheme and bribe to get what they want.

Will women ever get to the point where they support each other? They are the first to tear down each other. Women compare themselves with each other who looks better or wear name brand clothes. In some instances women will only associate with other women who they feel are in the same league with them eg. Class or looks.

Some women will laugh with their peers while sleeping with their men. They will convince themselves that something is wrong with the man's woman why he is sleeping with them. Of course men will play women into believing they are the true one.

Will women ever get to the point where there is true sisterhood? I don't know if we will ever see that in this lifetime, the world pitches women against each other. They like to see women bitch and fight each other. Women are branded as gossipers, emotional and the weaker sex. The image of women will not change until women decide that we need to change how we are viewed.

Sisterhood is something that has to be taken seriously and it has to start from our little girls. Little girls have to be taught to love themselves as they are. Not what anyone or society expect them to be. Whatever their flaws to learn to embrace them, while accentuating their strong points. If our little girls learn to appreciate themselves and their peers very early.
Growing up in a society that focuses on dividing and conquering women would not result in women bashing each other so often.

If women only learn how to tap into their special gifts we would have more women leaders. Women have always played a great deal in war and politics even if they were not at the forefront. Men depend on their sound judgment and initiative spirit. Women have an amount of strength that take them through trying times.

Can you imagine what this world would be like if women regardless of race or background bond together.

If women found the time to work together we could solve so many problems in our countries. We see the difference that powerful women have made Oprah, Mother Theresa, Margaret Thatcher, Bhoutos, Princess Diana to name a few. Therefore women should stop let the world dictate to us what their standards are.

It is time for women to step up, speak out and say Enough!. No more strife, no more bitchiness, no more cat fights. Let's love each other as women and support our sisters. As women we will all look different, some short, tall, lean, large does it matter. "NO IT DOESN'T". What matters is that women stop the strife.

Mama's Boy and Independent Woman

Mr. B and Marcia are basically from the same upbringing background from a single parent home. Marcia was taught to be independent and not to depend on others for anything. Mr. B was raised to be independent, sheltered from the outside world and to see his mother as his world and life. As a child, Mr. B mother told him no woman would ever love him like she does and when a woman say, "I love you" they are lying and don't mean it. Mr. B was not experience in relationships due to his insecurity about his weight and looks. He felt that no woman wanted him because he is too fat and he is not attractive enough for the average woman.

Marcia started working at the same company as Mr. B and they became friends after a few months and decided to start a relationship. Marcia didn't realize that Mr. B was a pathological liar and a manipulator but she went with the flow and ran with his inner personality. On their first date, they went to a Diner in mid Manhattan and watched the movie "The English Patient." On the second date he suggested they meet downtown at the Hotel Marina to spend time together as a couple. When Marcia arrived she was so impressed with the hotel and his effort to please her. They started to flirt with each other but Mr. B was very nervous because he was afraid she would have a problem with his weight and he fear he won't be able to please her. He was afraid to undress and so he stayed in his clothes while they made out. Marcia was very patient and assures him that she understands and will work with him so they both can be pleased and satisfied. Every time Mr. B put his wiener in her hot vagina, his wiener would shrink as if it was frighten by the hot well. Marcia decided she would help the brother out, so each time his wiener arise she would jump on him real quick to get a sensation before it falls. She did that for about thirty minutes till she was tired of the game,"jump on and off the wiener." As time goes by, the sex become better and better and Mr. B developed a talent for pussy sucking and became an expert at sucking the heck out of her hot well. The relationship has always been up and down due to his Mama who dictated his life and relationships.

Mr. B had rules for Marcia when it involves his mother:
* Do not come to my house unannounced or call his house at a certain time because he doesn't want her to wake up his mom.
* All Holidays are spent with his mother and only her.
* He cannot stay at her house pass 10pm because his mother may worry.
* They are only allowed to see each other on Saturdays, no weekdays or Sundays, those days are for his mother.

Marcia fell in love with Mr. B unconditionally; she dreamed of him, her life revolved around him, he was her knight and shining armor in her eyes. In his eyes, she was a piece of ass and the only person who wants him and would fuck him. There were times he would get cocky and start to say hurtful things to her such as; get a life, do not come to my house unless I invite you, can you massage my balls for me, can you suck my dick for me. Marcia felt as if she had to do these things to keep this man happy so he doesn't leave her. Her self esteem began to deteriote over the years with

Mr. B. their relationship was on and off, they broke up every six months and Marcia would date in between the breakups so she doesn't loose herself and her sanity. Most time when they have sex, she doesn't have an orgasm because he always make sure he came first and leave immediately and she would be left behind filled with her own frustration. The sexual fulfillment for him continued for years, it was all about him getting off, jacking off and she not getting a drop of her milk out. He became a sex selfish bastard and became too much of himself.

As the years fly by, Marcia became stronger and did some soul searching on her inner self. She took control of the sex and turned him inside out and started taking control of her own pussy. I guess you can say she did some pussy soul searching and brought it back to the surface. She controlled the sex and his wiener; she became the dick controller and tells him what to do to her sexually. She set him up on a schedule; he became her pussy and ass eater, buy her all her sex toys, woman porn magazine, sex tapes etc... They were times she wouldn't allow him to come for months but she always makes sure she came as many times as possible. Every week she would make sure he comes over to milk her well high and dry. Let me tell you Mr. B was a great pussy eater and sucker, he would suck that pussy till it is sore and the clit would be swollen from sucking for an hour or more. Marcia would call him and tell him what time, when to come drain her well, she wouldn't let him leave until he had fulfilled her sexual goals. He became her love slave without him knowing she was in control of his wiener and his luscious lips and tongue of wonders.

There were times in the relationship when Marcia and Mr. B had planned for the movies, his mother would pretend she was sick and make Mr. B feel guilty, so he would break his date with Marcia to cater to his mother. His mother asks him for grandchildren and he buys her two dogs (Trisha and Tristan) and told her these are her grandchildren. She treated those dogs as if they were her children and he would refer to the dogs as his brother and sister. The dogs even took on Mr. B and his mother personality. Trisha was bitchy and needy like his mother and Tristan was like Mr. B, overweight and greedy. Enough is enough, can you imagine competing with the dogs for a date, some good pussy licking and sucking and even some fucking.

If Marcia calls him to go shopping, he asks "can the dogs come too?", Marcia gets furious, "what the fuck", Hell to the fucking NO, I don't do Dogs man......

Mr. B took Marcia on a few vacations to Mexico all expense paid; she never had to contribute a dime. He was the best vacation partner; there is no arguing or disagrees but he still has that lying side to him. On vacations he would suck her pussy at least 4 times a day and all she has to do his massage his dick for him. It got to a point whereas he didn't care if he gets fucked; it was all about him sucking pussy. He became addicted to her pussy and sometimes he would call and ask if he can eat her pussy because he was hungry. She would refuse him because she wants it to be on her terms not his.

Till this day they are the best of friends but no intimate relationships between them. They can call upon each other for almost anything. Ladies you get a man who burn you one or too many times, you keep him as your best friend and he becomes your BITCH FORLIFE. The best part is he doesn't even know he is your BITCH.

CHARACTERS
Winston - 37 yrs old (Traditional Man)
Crystal- 34 yrs old (Independent Woman)
Karl - Winston Son
Darrel - Crystal Son
Lynn - Crystal Best Friend

Crystal

Crystal is an African American woman. She was born in Jamaica West Indies and lived there until the tender of eleven years old. She has four brothers and no sisters. She moved to New York with her mother and brother to Bronx, New York. At the age of 16 years old Crystal became pregnant and had to grow up fast to take care of her baby boy Darrel. Darrel was born in 1986, Bronx New York. Crystal had to work part time to support her baby; she also had to continue to finish high school. After high school she enrolled at Bronx Community College and graduated with an Associate degree in Human Services. Crystal have had several jobs to make ends meet such as Kentucky Fry Chicken (KFC), Caldor's Department Store, Alexander's Department Store, First Federal Bank and now work for a Retirement Insurance Company.

Crystal has had several problems on all her jobs but she still was able to maintain steadiness at her current job. In 1999, Crystal was given the opportunity to relocate to Denver Colorado with her company, which she was glad to accept because she needed a change in her life. Moving to Denver would give her an opportunity to grow within herself. She would be able to teach her son values, respect and independency to survive. Crystal move to Denver in 1999 with her son to start a new life. Crystal had a hard time adjusting to the new environment due to not having any friends or family in Colorado. Crystal had big goals for her self and her son. Her goal was to get her drivers license, buy a car, buy a house and return back to school to continue her education. Crystal was able to accomplish those goals by the year 2000.

Crystal had a difficult time making friends so she decided to turn to phone and online dating to make friends. She have met some really nice people whereas some were out of her range, worthless, controlling, leach and jack in the box type. She went out on several dates but still wasn't able to find
Mr. Right or sometimes she would say the man for her that God has intended for her to have was out there somewhere.

DECEMBER 28TH
It was a night of loneliness for a single independent woman. She was at home surfing the net hoping to find someone to talk to fulfill her gap of communication. As she was surfing the net, a message appear "You got mail". She opened the browser and read the email; it was from" dark and handsome" with a title" Come watch the sunset with me". His email states,

"I saw you online but I don't know how to connect with you. I am a traditional man and a man that knows how to treat a woman". She didn't respond to his email. He sends a second email, pleading for her to respond to him. She ignores the email again, thinking it's probably one of those guys who are seeking single women to take advantage of. A third email come through with the title "One more time", this message was attach with his phone number. She decided she will call him the following day. She didn't want him to think she was desperate to talk to someone.

The next day she called him and left a message for him to call her at work. The phone rang at work, she answered with a professional tone of voice. She recognized his voice and tells him, I know who you are and he responded "Who am I". She states, you are Winston. He was very impress that she was sharp. They both talked for a few minutes and decided to continue their conversation later. Later in the night Crystal was bored at home and decided to go for a drive to clear her mind. She calls Winston to say hello and chat for a bit. During the conversation Winston ask her to stop by his apartment. She agrees to stop by due to the fact that she had nothing planned for the night and she wanted to meet this mystery man. She asked him where he resides and he said, "Kennedy Ridge apartment complex," and she was so surprise because she once lived at the same complex.

She arrived at his apartment and he was outside waiting for her. She took one look at him and was not impressed with his looks but his politeness was appealing in her eyes. They both entered his apartment and he kept staring at her which scared her terribly. The conversation between them was very good and interesting because they found out they had a few things in common. She tried not to glance at him or have any eye contact. She was afraid of being attracted to him.

During the conversation, Winston asked her for her ring size and guesses it is maybe about a size 8. She laughed at his candid sense of humor. She started to think to herself; maybe he could be the one if she could just overlook his physical body and looks. Winston brought out his family photos and began to talk about how much family is important to him.

He proceeded to give an interview of himself such as, he loves women, he knows how to please a woman, and he knows what women want. The most interesting introduction was he carefully expressed he doesn't have a sexual identity disorder because he loves women. I ask him why he would mention the sexual identity, he replies people think he is gay because of his voice and the things he does because he does things differently to express himself. Crystal left the subject alone by not questioning it. After their long conversation, they both decided to end it and reside back to their life. She left feeling good because his personality was appealing and attractive but she still thinks he's not the type of man she usually date.

GIRL TALK

After meeting Winston, Crystal had to tell her friend Lynn about the mystery man. She explains to Lynn that Winston is not the type of man she usually dates. Lynn tells her maybe this is your blessing and don't let it get away from you.

THE PROPOSAL

Their conversation continued for a few days and it became more in depth. They discuss their dreams and desire for life. He portrays himself as a kind, loving, affectionate, caring and a family man. She described herself to him as an independent, strong minded, outspoken, caring and goal oriented woman. They also discuss the desire of wanting to be married and having a family life. The discussion continues with wanting to have a child together. She became very impress and began to like him as a person and she looked more on the inside rather than the outside.

Suddenly, he asked her to marry him and she ignored his gesture of proposal of marriage. He repeats it again, "Will you marry me Crystal?" She was surprise but overwhelmed of negative thoughts of is it a joke or his he for real. She told him she can't give him an answer yet, she needs time to think about it. He told her he will give her the time but he won't wait no longer than six months. He also suggested that they won't have sex until they are married because he wants to respect her body. She is thinking to herself, he better be good in bed, or else he has to go or enroll in the "How to please school" better yet the "How to fuck school." Days went by and he was still proposing to her but no ring insight. She didn't worry about the ring because she was more impressed with him as a person. She finally decided, what the hell this only happen once in a lifetime.

She decided one day to text him with the message "Yes, I will marry you" but she warned him she is not in love with him and she takes marriage very seriously. He was very overjoyed and excited. He decided to call his mother and give her the good news of his new beginning. She was very hesitant in alerting her family of her new life to be started.

Winston was very excited about the thought of getting married. He would call Crystal every chance he get to tell her how much he love her, how he needs her in his life, he is so happy and he knows they will be both happy together. Whenever he expresses himself she would just listen and be jittery with laughter and sudden happiness of disbelief that this can't be happening to her. Winston would quiz Crystal on life experience to see where she is at with her thoughts or maybe he was just trying to see how far he can go to capture her heart. Crystal would still have her radar up about Winston because she felt this was too good to be true. One day Winston call Crystal and had his mother on a 3 way call for his mother to give her blessing which she did. Crystal started to believe he must be for real because which man would be kidding and go to the extreme of asking his mother for her blessing.

On a cold Monday evening, Crystal stopped by Winston's resident for a visit. He suggested they go to the mall where his son would also join them. They arrived at the mall as a family, walked around for awhile. Winston gave his son some money for the arcade while he and Crystal walked around the mall. They came upon a

Jewelry store (Jake's Jewelry) and Winston looks around at the jewelries in the show case. Crystal thinks to herself if he knows the type of ring she likes, then it will confirm he is the one for her. Suddenly, he asked the salesman "Can you point me to the Ruby's". Crystal was in shock but happy that he knew what she wants. He asks the salesman to measure her ring size which is 8 %. Crystal asks him, "How did you know the type of ring I want?" He replies I always know what you want. Crystal heart grows more and more in belief and thought to her self, "I finally found my prince charming". Winston picks out her ring which was a simple gold engagement ring and band with a ruby stone. Crystal got a little jittery and excited this is finally for real. Her feelings for Winston became more real and secure.

THE ANNOUNCEMENT

Crystal and Winston decided to make the announcement to their kids. Winston decided to make the announcement to his son about his new life. He told Karl, he has met a woman, the woman of his dream. He explains to his son, this woman would be like a mother to him and he wants him to accept her. His son replies, "Yes dad, I'm happy for you". Winston was very please Karl was accepting of this new beginning plus, he was glad his father is happy again.

Winston and Crystal decided to break the news to Crystal son, Darrel. Darrel was at the dining table eating dinner. Crystal introduced Winston and his son Karl to Darrel. Darrel politely but uncover rudely gesture hello to both parties. Crystal looked at Darrel's eyes and sees the despair and anger through his eyes and body language. She knew right away he doesn't approve of Winston. Darrell suddenly rushes up to his room and slammed the door.

Winston senses the vibe of uninvited welcome. He told Crystal he should depart because he felt that Darrel does not approve of him and he felt a bit uncomfortable.

Crystal decided to have a one on one talk with her son. She told him she will be marrying Winston and Darrel was highly upset. He dash off to his room and said, "How dare you are going to get married and not asked my approval." Crystal responded to him, "Who are you for me to ask permission to be married." She tries to explain things to him and he gesture for her to get out of his room and that he doesn't want to talk to her right now.

Two weeks went by, Crystal and her son was still on non speaking terms. Crystal was ok with it because she decided she is going to be happy and live her life the way she wants to live it. Crystal and Darrel kept their distance form each other by cutting off all communication. Crystal would sleep at Winston house at least 3 times a week to avoid conflict with Darrel. As Crystal slept out more often, Darrel would start to call her at work and on her cell checking to see where she is.

Darrel was afraid of loosing his mother to another man because it has always been both them through thick and thin. Crystal does understand Darrel feelings but she feels he has to learn to let go and let her live her life.

THE WEDDING PLANS

The weddings plans had began. They both were excited about the wedding plans and the thought of being a family. Winston took it upon himself to start the wedding arrangements which was unusual for a man to do. They both had previously discussed the date which would be on May 23rd and the colors of the wedding theme (Ruby and Amethyst). Winston went to the Red Velvet and made arrangements for the wedding to surprise Crystal. After he left the Red Velvet he calls Crystal in despair and sounding confuse. She tries to calm him down and tell him it will be ok soon. He expresses how much he loves her dearly and he is so happy. Few days later, he confesses to her he had made the arrangements for the wedding and paid for the down payment for the wedding ceremony and reception. She was so impress but yet in disbelief that he could actually be for real. She told him she wants to see proof that he actually made these plans on his own.

The next day they both went to the Red Velvet to confirm he made the wedding arrangements. They entered the premises and the Host greeted them delightfully and pleasantly. He introduced himself and proceeded to show Crystal the paper work of the contract Winston had signed.
Crystal was so impress with Winston of making the arrangements on his own. She starts to believe him more and more each day but she still continues to keep her radar alert and active.

Days went on and their relationship seem to blossoming each day. Crystal starts to get in the mood of actually being soon to be married. Winston become more and more believable each day. Crystal decided to make the announcement to people by calling her family and friends one day at a time but instructing them not to ask any questions about this mystery man. Everyone was in disbelief Crystal would even get married but they didn't say anything to her. The most difficult phone call was to call her mother and invite her to her wedding. The call to her mother went very well because for the first time her mother was very happy for her and was in approval of her getting married. Winston continues to be loving and supportive towards Crystal. Crystal began to love Winston and she expresses her feeling to him which made him very happy.

THE FIRST SEXUAL ENCOUNTER CHOPPER STYLE

One Sunday night Winston called Crystal and asked her to spend the night at his apartment. She packed her overnight bag and proceeded to spending the night with her future. She cuddles in bed with him and their bodies caressed each other. He asked her to undress and she reply, "I thought we were going to wait untill we get married." Winston says, "Yes, we will but we are just going to enjoy each other's body." They proceeded to cuddle and caress each other. He kissed her from her fore head and proceeded to the middle of her luscious body. He compliments her on how sexy she is and he is so turned on by her heated body and he wanted her sexually. She agreed to have him enter her because she hasn't had sex in a few months and her body was yearning for passion.

He goes down to the center of her body below the hip and began to lick the outside of her almond pond. As he was licking her, she started to feel real good but not the way she wanted to feel. Winston proceeded to lick the clit, her weak spot but it didn't seem appealing to her. His licking become annoying but she just stood still pretending to enjoy his licking. He then positioned her missionary style to enter his chopper in her almond pond, she thinks to herself, this is not going to work but continues to pretend. He pounded her with his chopper as if he was doing a great job. She suddenly told him, "Honey, I like it doggy style".

He positioned her big round almond melon ass up in the air back ways, ready to get chopped up by chopper. He rammed her in and out but still no passion felt. He had no motion in her ocean, no ghetto in the valley, she was so disappointed because she thought he was going to blow her mind wide open with passion. He shoots his soldiers up her dry river till she felt them running for dear life. It felt as if one of the soldiers must have gotten stuck on his way up the dry river. After he was done with his fail test drive, she told him she wasn't able to produce fruit juice and her Niagara Falls ran dry. He had the nerves to reply, "You are too independent that's why you didn't cry a river." She was highly upset because she realized that the mother fucker can't fuck for his dear life.

One day she decided to examine chopper to see why he didn't perform well that night. She had Winston lay on his back exposing his manhood. As she checked his dark chocolate body which was very sexy and appealing. She proceeded to work her way down to chopper and turned him towards the light. He was big, fat and a nice length which seem big and wide width enough to please a woman. Crystal examines the tip of chopper and it seems look able, tasty and juicy. As she focused her eyes on the center of chopper she noticed it looked a bit unusual.

Chopper looked a little chopped up chopper style. She began to feel disgusted with the look of chopper. It had brown and black stripes like it was painted or camouflage with bad decoration. She asked him, "Honey, what happen to chopper?" He replies, "I got circumcised." She says, are you sure because it looked like a homicide and maybe we need to file a complaint for destruction of property chopper style? She decided there is no way that chopper will be allowed to be exposed in her presence or in her tunnel because chopper needs treatment for damages.

It was then and there that she decided to run. She did not want any nutty buddy or chop chop. One word came to her "run". She said, "Winston honey, it was nice knowing you." He looked a bit shocked. "Why?" he asked.
"Your goods are damaged property, and it just won't do." She walked out of his house and his life and never looked back.

Ladies make sure you know what you are getting before you take up a man. After all, you can get perfect plastic on batteries that feel like the real thing and in many instances, do a better job why then settle for less.

Dating Scene

The black guy at the gas station, well I did try to get to know him to see if my instinct was wrong about him. After talking to him a few times, I was getting the feeling that I don't want to go out with him. One day he called and told me the next day we will go out for a walk. Next day came no call, but I wasn't worried because I was more focus on my school work. He didn't call for the walk which was supposed to be at 6pm. He called around 9:30pm to talk but I didn't answer, he left message. I call back and left a message stating, how I enjoyed the beautiful walk we took. How enjoyable, breath taking and the talk we had was great. He call the next day stating how he thought my message was funny, I told him I wasn't joking I was serious. I went on an imaginary mental walk with him that date and time. The only thing was, he wasn't there. He was like, that is not like me to do that. I was like, don't worry brother, it was the best walk ever. Girl, what he doesn't realize is this doesn't faze me at all.

Anyway the weekend was his birthday and he wanted us to go out on a date. I was thinking to myself I hope this idiot wasn't expecting me to buy him a gift because we ain't like that yet, or never. I kept getting this feeling that this is not right for me to go out with him. I say to myself, listen to your instinct and go with it. So I told him I don't want to mess up his day and he should enjoy it alone and not with me. He was like you sound like you don't want to go. I am saying to myself, I have dealt with you all black men before so I know the rope and I ain't going there. We end up not going and chatted on the phone for a while. I always say when you meet a guy and he seems too nice and within your taste, listen to him carefully because he sure will mess up soon. This guy kept going on how he is a mamas boy, he is a Christian and he love the Lord but in the same sentence he mentioned he used to sell, smoke weed back in college and continue to say he occasionally smoke weed. I was like back the fuck up, what did you just say about Jesus and weed in the same sentence, he repeated. I told him straight up listen, I'm totally against people who smoke weed at his age (44 years old), that is not my thing at all and I can't be around people who engage in such activities. He states that I sound like he is trying to sell me weed. I told him this is something I'm against and I stand my ground on it. I have been there with men like him and they don't grow out of it. Girl, I was immediately turned off from him and I think he picked it up in my voice. He told me he can hear it in my voice and silence. Whatever Asshole..

Then he had the nerve to compare people listening to different types of music because of their taste. I was like, this is two different categories and it cannot be compared. My thing is when do they grow out of it (weed smoking at such a late age). The dam idiot thinks it is normal.
Is he holding the Bible in one hand and the weed in the other, as he says AMEN, he take a draw of the spliff.

Though you would enjoy this story. I'm over these black men. I will send another email because I had a date today with a white guy.

Email: fedup146@hotmail.com

The Other Woman

Slut! Whore! Home wrecker! You name it, the other woman gets it. But who is to be blame in this type of relationship? It would seem as if the other woman (the mistress) gets the blame. In many instances it is the men who pursue these women and when she tries to leave the man refuses to let go. Many men will tell women stories of their marriage not working or things they dislike. They may say they can't leave because of the children or because of financial reasons. They want to have their cake and eat it. On the other hand, there are the men who tell these women that they love their wife and children and have no intention of leaving their family.

The question then remains, why do women enter into these relationships and why is it that society seems to blame the women? Do the men not have a stake in this? Are they not to take some of the responsibility and be made accountable? The thing in this type of relationship you may have different arrangements and it depends on the parties who enter into it. Let's look at some scenarios.

Cherrie is a 35 year old Psychologist and her friend is a 31 year old Pilot. They are very close and they have a BFB relationship (Best Friends with Benefit). They sleep together and share their emotions. Cherrie is independent but tries not to get attached. They both insist that nothing is to ever spoil their friendship. This seems to work for them.

Vicky who is 43 years old on the other hand, is involved with someone who pays all her bills and caters to her needs. She speaks of him as if the two of them are together as man and wife. She waits on him to make decisions for her. Even though she is the other woman, her actions and speech dictate otherwise. She prepares his food and fusses over him. When asked what if something happens to the man, how she copes, she shrugs it off because she doesn't want to deal with it, this arrangement suits her.

Then you have the women who are solely in it for the financial means. These are normally independent strong women, they normally have a goal. Tesha is one such woman. She sent herself to school to become a Lawyer, bought an apartment and a nice car. She knows this relationship will never go anywhere but that's okay, she has her independence and she has achieved what she has set out to do.

There is the second type of women who enters this relationship for financial means in order to live a certain lifestyle. This is the high maintenance woman who wears brand name and has her hair and nails done weekly. Normally, this type woman has nothing to show and is only in the relationship for security. Marcia has been with Jeff for 10 years and has two children for him. He maintains both her and the children. These women in some instances will have a child even though the man is married, just to maintain their status quo.

The last type of women is those who really believe the man will eventually leave their wife for them. The man tells them different stories why they can't leave and they hang on waiting for this moment. Antoinette has been with a man for 5 years and she believes that when the time is right he will leave his wife for her. These types of women will call wives and harass them because they think that they are standing between them and the man. Years come and go and the relationship remains the same.

When all is said and done it cannot be the women alone who is to be blamed. The men should be called some of the terrible names and take their share of the blame. Truth is, the "Other Woman" has been around for many centuries. I don't think it is going to end anytime soon. Maybe this is the reason why some cultures allow a man to have more than one wife. I have often wondered why is it that men feel the need to have more than woman. Why then marry? But then again is it possible for a man to only stick to one partner? Are they genetically wired to stray?

These questions cannot be answered simple. Hopefully, with more research in time we will get the answers needed. In the meantime, the punishment must fit the crime. If both parties are involved, then both must be equally blamed and suffer the consequences. The men are "Punks, Pricks, Home wreckers" call it as it is seen.

Pum-Pum Wars
(Or Confessions of a Former "Other Woman")

I prefer to think of it in terms of a war of the pum-pums, rather than wife versus the other woman. Seriously, when you get right down to the meat of the matter (pun intended), it boils down to (1) man not getting enough pum-pum at home; (2) man tired of pum-pum at home and therefore (3) man wants to try new pum-pum.

I am not sure which of these three scenarios led to my being cast in the role of the other woman. I never thought of it then as the war of the pum-pums. So I never asked him what the home pum-pum situation was like. However, having played that role for a while, I have had time to reflect on the situation and have some sisterly advice and confessions for those seriously considering this adventure, or for those who are currently occupying the role of the other woman.

Looking back now, I want to kick myself for having been the other woman, and therefore unwittingly being drawn into the pum-pum war. You see, my self esteem was low in those early years and any attention from the opposite sex was welcomed. Now, I know so much better. The guy in question turned out to be a real you know what. And to think that he benefited from, and enjoyed my sweet pum-pum all those years makes me cringe. He was, in fact, having the best of both worlds, because whatever his home pum-pum situation was, he was enjoying mine as well. Bastard. He was also an egotistical jerk who was no fun to be with because he was always so worried about being caught as a participant in the pum-pum war. Imagine a guy worried about your taking a photo of him because he wasn't sure who might be looking in your photo album one of these days! Or, can you believe he got annoyed at my writing "I love you" with lipstick on a hotel's bathroom mirror, on another continent from where he lives, because, as he puts it "you never know?" How utterly unromantic!

So, take it from a been there sister. Keep your pum-pum to yourself. Or better yet, find your own man, despite all the challenges that may come. At least you can relax, half-knowing no one else has a claim on him. But a girl can never be totally sure, right?

NOTES

NOTES

NOTES

NOTES

NOTES

NOTES